C I T Y P A C K
Atlanta

By Mark Beffart

2ND EDITION

Fodor's Travel Publications, Inc.
New York • Toronto • London • Sydney • Auckland

WWW.FODORS.COM/

Contents

About this book

KEY TO SYMBOLS

✝ map reference on the fold-out map accompanying this book (see below)

✉ address

☎ telephone number

🕐 opening times

🍴 restaurant or café on premises or nearby

Ⓜ nearest metro (underground) train station

🚆 nearest overground train station

🚌 nearest bus route

🚢 nearest riverboat or ferry stop

♿ facilities for visitors with disabilities

✋ admission charge

⬌ other nearby places of interest

❓ tours, lectures, or special events

➤ indicates the page where you will find a fuller description

ℹ tourist information

Citypack Atlanta is divided into six sections to cover the six most important aspects of your visit to Atlanta. It includes:

- The author's view of the city and its people
- Itineraries, walks and excursions
- The top 25 sights to visit—as selected by the author
- Features on what makes the city special
- Detailed listings of restaurants, hotels, shops and nightlife
- Practical information

In addition, easy-to-read side panels provide extra facts and snippets, highlights of places to visit, and invaluable practical advice.

CROSS-REFERENCES

To help you make the most of your visit, cross-references, indicated by ➤, show you where to find additional information about a place or subject.

MAPS

- The fold-out map in the wallet at the back of the book is a comprehensive street plan of Atlanta. All the map references given in the book refer to this map. For example, the State Capitol of Georgia at 206 Washington Street has the following information: ✝ F7—indicating the grid square of the map in which the State Capitol will be found.
- The city-center maps found on the inside front and back covers of the book itself are for quick reference. They show the Top 25 Sights, described on pages 24–48, which are clearly plotted by number (❶ – ㉕, not page number) from south to north across the city.

PRICES

Where appropriate, an indication of the cost of an establishment is given by $ signs: **$$$** denotes higher prices, **$$** denotes average prices, while **$** denotes lower charges.

ATLANTA *life*

INTRODUCING ATLANTA

Beckoning city

Your first sight of Atlanta's modern skyline, especially if you enter the city from the south or north, is truly magnificent. As you reach the crest of a hill, it appears like a beacon, towers of varying sizes and shapes gleaming in the sunlight and jabbing at the sky to form a dramatic symbol of Atlanta's success.

Downtown Atlanta

In 1959, in the heat of the Civil Rights debates, Mayor William B. Hartsfield proudly called Atlanta "the city too busy to hate." Two years later, while blacks were still being arrested in demonstrations across the South, Atlanta became the first southern city to desegregate its schools peacefully.

This slogan marks the essence of Atlanta's history. It has always been a busy city, not willing to remain in the past, but moving forward at a rapid rate, shrewd entrepreneurs adding to the success of their predecessors. After 90 percent of Atlanta was destroyed (1864) in the Civil War, it was quickly rebuilt, becoming a "brave and beautiful city" as noted in 1886 by *Atlanta Constitution* editor Henry Grady.

Today, its nicknames of Hotlanta, The Big A, Capital of the New South, and the International Gateway City, along with its distinctive modern skyline, evoke visions of a dynamic and progressive city. As you fly over Atlanta, a vast city spreads out in all directions, evidence of a phenomenal growth rate that has seen the population double since 1975, when it was called the five county metropolitan area by the Chamber of Commerce. Today it boasts over 3 million people living in over 20 counties that encompass 6,150 square miles and 111 suburban towns—and it is still expanding.

Come to Atlanta expecting to be greatly surprised. The Old South, as dramatized by the novel and movie *Gone with the Wind*, doesn't exist here. As a result of several public relations campaigns, Atlanta has attracted people from every state and numerous foreign

Inside the Fox Theatre

countries. This fusion of ardent southerners and new neighbors gives the city a unique character, a combination of southern charm and a dose of northern brashness and worldly sophistication. Atlanta is not a typical southern city, slow and backward as portrayed by Hollywood. The pace here is fast, easily attested from the moment you enter the multilane interstate highway system that crisscrosses and circles the city.

Despite its pace, Atlanta is a fun and hospitable place to visit. From walking tours in its beautiful neighborhoods, to visits to historical sights and high-tech attractions, to restaurants encompassing every possible cuisine, to a vibrant entertainment scene with Broadway theater, music concerts, ballet, and professional sports, there is no room for boredom here. Atlanta is a city with something for everyone.

International immigration

The signs of Atlanta's progress are visible everywhere. For proof of its growth as an international city, look to the suburb of Chamblee, located a short distance southwest of the I-85/I-285 intersection. Fifteen years ago, this community had a primarily white-only, working-class population. Today, it has one of the largest Asian communities in the United States.

ATLANTA IN FIGURES

GENERAL INFORMATION

- Atlanta is 1,050 feet above sea level, the highest elevation of any major U.S. city east of the Mississippi River
- The highest point in Atlanta is on Peachtree Street between Ellis Street and International Boulevard
- Atlanta is located 33°45'10" latitude north, approximately level with North Africa
- Atlanta is the ninth largest metropolitan area in the United States, with over 3.4 million people, yet only 422,427 people (1995 census) live within the Atlanta city limits, making it the 30th largest city
- The Atlanta metropolitan area consists of 6,150 square miles, 20 counties, and 111 suburban towns
- Sixty-four percent of Atlantans own their own home and land
- The average Atlanta resident takes 56 minutes to commute from home to place of employment
- African-Americans comprise approximately 65 percent of the Atlanta city population
- Over 95,000 students attend Atlanta's 42 colleges, universities, technical institutes, and seminaries
- None of the famous movie *Gone with the Wind* was filmed in Georgia

ATLANTA COMMERCE

- Underground Atlanta is Atlanta's most popular tourist attraction, with over 13 million annual visitors
- Seven hundred thirty of the *Fortune* 1,000 companies have offices in Atlanta
- More than 1,200 foreign businesses operate in Atlanta, and 48 countries have representation through consulates and trade offices
- Sales tax on most retail goods and services is 5–6 percent in Atlanta, 4–5 percent in the suburbs
- Lenox Square Mall is the largest enclosed shopping mall in the South, with over 14 million annual visitors
- Fifty percent of Georgia's physicians practice medicine in the metropolitan Atlanta area

ATLANTA PEOPLE

HANK AARON (b. 1934)

Baseball star Hank Aaron is Atlanta's most famous professional athlete. On April 8, 1974, this Atlanta Braves outfielder claimed his place in sports history by hitting home run number 715, which broke the record held by Babe Ruth for 37 years. "The Hammer," or "Hammering Hank," as he was known during his career, went on to hit another 40 home runs before he retired from active playing in 1976. He is also the all-time leader for runs batted in (2,297), second in runs scored (2,174), and third in hits (3,771). In 1982, his first year of eligibility, he was elected to the Baseball Hall of Fame. Today, he is a vice president of the Braves.

JIMMY CARTER (b. 1924)

After a brief term as a state legislator in the 1960s, Jimmy Carter, a peanut farmer from the south central Georgia town of Plains, became the 76th governor of Georgia in 1971. Five years later, in November 1976, he was elected as the 39th President of the United States. Although he was unable to solve all of the country's problems during his administration (1977–1981), his work afterwards with Habitat for Humanity and the Carter Presidential Center (► 35) has thrust him into the spotlight. Today he is in demand as a peace negotiator (in recent years concerning the conflicts in Korea, Bosnia, Haiti, and various African nations) and a conference speaker.

CORETTA SCOTT KING (b. 1928)

The widow of Martin Luther King, Jr. has done more than anyone to further the legacy and philosophy of the slain Civil Rights leader. Shortly after his 1968 assassination in Memphis, Tennessee, she established the Martin Luther King, Jr. Center for Non-Violent Social Change, which is visited by thousands of people every year who come to view King's tomb and to attend conferences on various Civil Rights and black culture topics. She is active in many Civil Rights organizations and has traveled the world to promote her husband's ideas.

Ted Turner

Ted Turner (b.1938)

Atlanta's richest man is known as a "maverick" and a "gambler." Ignoring his critics, he parlayed an inheritance from his father's billboard company in the late 1960s to create a small independent television station (TBS). Today it is billed as the "Superstation," and is one of the most profitable cable stations in the U.S. In the mid-1970s Turner bought a major-league baseball team (Braves) and a basketball team (Hawks), which he still owns. In the 1980s, after failing to buy one of the primary television networks, he carved out his own media empire by creating the 24-hour news network CNN, followed by Headline News, and several other cable networks. He also owns 6,700 MGM movies. In 1996 he merged all of his television business with the media conglomerate Time Warner, becoming Vice President for them in the process.

A CHRONOLOGY

1782   British explorers discover the Creek village of Standing Indian at the confluence of the Chattahoochee River and Peachtree Creek

1812   Fort Gilmer, a Federal militia outpost, is established at Standing Indian

1826   Surveyors suggest the Atlanta area for a railroad to connect the state with northern markets

1833   Hardy Ivy, Atlanta's first permanent settler, builds a log cabin on the present-day site of Courtland and Ellis Streets (Downtown)

1837   Stephen H. Long, a military engineer, marks the terminus of the state-owned Western Atlantic Railroad with the "Zero Milepost," and a tiny village named Terminus begins to grow

1843   Terminus is renamed Marthasville after popular ex-Governor Wilson Lumpkin's daughter Martha

1845   Marthasville is renamed Atlanta

1847   Atlanta is officially incorporated as a city

1860   Atlanta's population reaches 10,000

1861   Georgia secedes from the Union and joins the Confederacy

1864   Union armies under General William Tecumseh Sherman lay siege to Atlanta for two months, destroying 90 percent of the city

1868   Atlanta becomes the capital of Georgia

1870   Georgia is readmitted into the Union, the last seceded Confederate state to gain re-entry

1886   Pharmacist John S. Pemberton creates a new headache remedy called Coca-Cola

1900   Professor E. B. DuBois founds the National Association for the Advancement of Colored People (NAACP). Population is now 90,000

1917	A fire destroys 1,938 buildings, making 10,000 people homeless and claiming one fatality
1920	Atlanta's population grows to 200,000
1929	Atlanta opens its first airport, Candler Field
1936	Margaret Mitchell's novel *Gone with the Wind* is published; over 1 million copies are sold by the year's end
1939	The movie of *Gone with the Wind* premieres in Atlanta at the Loews Grand Theater; black cast members and other blacks are not allowed to attend due to segregation laws
1959	Sit-ins, boycotts, and riots protesting the segregation of blacks from white schools and other establishments begin in Atlanta
1964	Martin Luther King, Jr. wins the Nobel Prize for Peace. The Beatles perform at Atlanta Stadium
1966	The Braves major-league baseball franchise moves to Atlanta from Milwaukee. The Falcons National Football League team begins its first year in Atlanta
1968	The funeral of assassinated Martin Luther King, Jr. is held in Atlanta
1971	Jimmy Carter is elected Governor of Georgia
1974	Maynard Jackson is elected Atlanta's first black mayor
1979	MARTA Rapid Rail (subway-elevated train system) opens for business
1983	Martin Luther King, Jr.'s birthday becomes a national holiday
1988	Atlanta hosts the Democratic National Convention
1996	Atlanta hosts the 26th Summer Olympics

PEOPLE & EVENTS FROM HISTORY

The Battle of Atlanta, 1864

SIEGE OF ATLANTA IN 1864

The Union army laid siege to Atlanta from July 22 to August 22. The heaviest bombardment occurred in the period August 9–11 as eleven Union batteries and ten Confederate units fought against one another. During this period, the city was an inferno as over 5,000 shells struck it, reducing it to rubble. One onlooker wrote that "…all the fires of hell, and all the thunders of the universe seemed to be blazing and roaring over Atlanta." Amazingly, only 20 citizens were killed during the shelling.

THE COCA-COLA COMPANY

The most renowned beverage in the world was originally developed as a headache remedy in 1886 by pharmacist John S. Pemberton. Frank Robinson, one of Pemberton's partners, crafted the famous script still used in its trademark and named the drink after its two primary ingredients, the coca leaf and kola nut. Pemberton could not foresee its potential and subsequently sold the formula to Asa Candler in 1891 for $2,300. A merchandizing wizard, Candler developed Coca-Cola into Atlanta's most prosperous company, selling it for $25 million in 1919 to a group headed by Ernest Woodruff.

ASSASSINATION OF MARTIN LUTHER KING, JR.

When Martin Luther King, Jr. was assassinated in 1968, black neighborhoods broke into riots across the nation. As Atlanta prepared for the funeral, they also prepared for violence, an act King preached against. Mayor Ivan Allen was instructed by Robert Woodruff, the President of Coca-Cola, to do whatever was right and necessary to honor the slain leader, Woodruff promising to absorb whatever costs the city could not handle. Over 200,000 people, black and white, rich and poor, celebrities and the unknown, marched in the funeral procession.

Andrew Young (b.1932)

Since the assassination of Martin Luther King, Jr. in 1968, a number of black leaders have picked up the torch of the Civil Rights movement. In Atlanta, Andrew Young is the most prominent. In 1972, he became the first black member of the U.S. Congress since the late 1860s, serving until 1977 when he was named Ambassador to the United Nations. In 1981, he became Mayor of Atlanta, a post he held until 1989. As a consummate promoter, he has done more than any other person in the past 20 years to bring worldwide attention to Atlanta.

ATLANTA
how to organize your time

ITINERARIES

Atlanta is a sprawling city that is best divided into smaller sections for touring. For easy division, spend a day visiting the sights near each of its three main business districts: Downtown, Midtown, and Buckhead, all accessible by public transportation. Then explore some of the city's interesting neighborhoods and suburban sights.

ITINERARY ONE	DOWNTOWN
	Downtown Atlanta contains some of the city's most interesting sights and attractions
Breakfast	Start with an early breakfast at your hotel
Morning	Visit the State Capitol of Georgia (➤ 27) Walk down Martin Luther King, Jr. Drive to The World of Coca-Cola (➤ 28). Cross Depot Plaza to Underground Atlanta (➤ 29)
Lunch	Dine at Mick's (➤ 63), at No. 75 on the Upper Alabama Street level
Afternoon	Visit Atlanta Heritage Row (➤ 30) and the Olympic Experience (➤ 29). From Five Points station, take the MARTA train to the CNN Center (➤ 31)
ITINERARY TWO	MIDTOWN
	Midtown is the cultural center of Atlanta, with the city's art museum and famed Fox Theatre
Breakfast	Have doughnuts and coffee at Krispy Kreme, 295 Ponce de Leon Avenue
Morning	Exit left, and walk a half mile or take bus 2 to Peachtree Street. Turn right to Road to Tara Museum (➤ 42) and Fox Theatre (➤ 41) across the street. Behind Fox Theatre enter the modern building to Telephone Museum (➤ 54)
Lunch	The Varsity (➤ 63), Atlanta's most famous cheap eatery, is only three blocks from here
Afternoon	Take train from North Avenue station to Arts Center (N5) for High Museum of Art (➤ 43) Walk through Ansley Park neighborhood (➤ 58) for 1 mile or take a taxi to Atlanta Botanical Garden (➤ 44)

ITINERARY THREE	BUCKHEAD
	Buckhead is a favorite area with Atlantans for shopping, dining, and partying
Breakfast	Coffee and pastries at Café Intermezzo Coffeehouse (145 Peachtree Road)
Morning	Explore the art galleries, antiques, and decorative furnishings stores along Bennett Street (➤ 72) Take bus 23 to Pharr Road. Walk down Pharr Road to Oxford Books (➤ 74). Turn left on Buckhead Avenue, behind the store, to reach Fay Gold Gallery (➤ 73). Cross to Bolling Way, lined with clubs, to reach East Paces Ferry Road, also lined with clubs, stores, and galleries
Lunch	Take bus 40 to Atlanta History Center (➤ 46) and dine at the Coach House Restaurant there (🕐 11:30–2:30)
Afternoon	Tour Atlanta History Center sights Take bus 40 or 58 to Georgia Governor's Mansion (➤ 47). Return to Peachtree Street and take bus 23 to Lenox Square Mall
ITINERARY FOUR	ATLANTA NEIGHBORHOODS
	Atlanta's sights are spread all over the city, some dispersed within its beautiful neighborhoods
Breakfast	M.O.C.H.A. coffee-house, 1424 North Highland Avenue (near University Drive)
Morning	Follow North Highland Avenue or take bus 16 through the chic Virginia-Highland neighborhood (➤ 58) to the Carter Presidential Center—about 2 miles (➤ 35). Little Five Points (➤ 18) is a ten-minute walk from here. Walk down Euclid Avenue to Inman Park (➤34)
Lunch	Dine at Burton's Grill (➤ 62)
Afternoon	Take MARTA to the Candler Park station and bus 6 to Michael C. Carlos Museum (➤ 48) Follow Clifton Road to the Fernbank Museum of Natural History (➤ 36)

WALKS

INFORMATION

Distance 4 miles

Time 40–60 minutes (no stops);
2–4 hours to take time to
view inside buildings and
sights

Start point Underground Atlanta

➕ F7

✉ Peachtree Street at Upper
Alabama Street

Ⓜ Five Points (0)

End point Midtown

➕ F5

✉ Peachtree Street at North
Avenue

Ⓜ North Avenue (N3)

PEACHTREE STREET:
DOWNTOWN

Since Atlanta's original charter, Peachtree Street
has been the spine and major thoroughfare of
the city. Beginning at Underground Atlanta,
follow it north to Five Points, the heart of
Atlanta's financial district, named after the
convergence of Peachtree Street (twice, N and
S), Decatur Street (E), Marietta Street (W), and
Edgewood Avenue (NE). At the Marietta corner
is the 43-story Wachovia Bank of Georgia
Tower, situated on the site of Jacob's Drug Store
where Coca-Cola was first served as a fountain
drink in 1886. Georgia State University, a few
blocks to the east, contains the Mercer Music
Collection. A half block north on Peachtree
Street is the newly landscaped Woodruff Park,
with the 52-story, rusty colored Georgia-Pacific
Building in the background. A right turn on to
Auburn Avenue, at the top of the park, leads to
the Martin Luther King, Jr. National Historic
District.

Business, shopping, and culture Continuing
north on Peachtree Street, take a look at the
triangular Flatiron Building and elaborately
decorated Candler Building. Opposite the latter
is the High Museum of Art Folk Art and
Photography Galleries in the Georgia-Pacific
Building. To the left across Peachtree Street is
the tiny Margaret Mitchell Park and the cubist-
looking Atlanta-Fulton County Public Library.
Ahead is the shiny 73-story cylindrical Westin
Peachtree Plaza Hotel and the One Ninety One
Peachtree Tower with its funky neoclassical top.
At opposite Ellis Street corners, peep into the
luxurious Ritz-Carlton Hotel and Macy's
department store. For an early lunch, stop at the
Hard Rock Cafe (Peachtree Street at Inter-
national Boulevard) or one of many restaurants a
half block farther north at The Mall at the
Peachtree Center. One block left (west) via
International Boulevard is the new Welcome
South Center, with tourist bureaux for eight
southern states, a travel bookstore, and a
Thomas Cook foreign-exchange office.

PEACHTREE STREET: MIDTOWN

Continue to walk north along Peachtree Street past the Hyatt Regency Atlanta Hotel to Ralph McGill Boulevard, where you can either turn right to reach SciTrek or continue straight on to the Atlanta Museum. Ahead on the left is the NationsBank Plaza Tower, the tallest building in the South. If you haven't had lunch yet, turn left on North Avenue and walk for two blocks to The Varsity. A little farther along Peachtree Street is the Fox Theatre and Road to Tara Museum.

Between 5th and 10th Streets You will find that this area is rather seedy and the primary turf of prostitutes, so you may want to take the train from the North Avenue station to the Midtown station (N4), exiting right to Peachtree Street. Between 10th and 14th Streets are several new skyscrapers that rival the Downtown skyline. Just past 15th Street is the Woodruff Arts Center, home to the Atlanta Symphony and Alliance Theatre, and next door is the modern High Museum of Art.

THE SIGHTS

- SciTrek (➤ 39)
- Atlanta Museum (➤ 40)
- NationsBank Plaza Tower (➤ 51)
- The Varsity (➤ 63)
- Fox Theatre (➤ 41)
- Road to Tara Museum (➤ 42)
- Woodruff Arts Center
- High Museum of Art (➤ 43)

INFORMATION

Distance 3 miles
Time 40 minutes (no stops); 2–3 hours to take time to view inside buildings and sights
Start point Midtown (where walk can be divided)
🚻 F5
✉ Peachtree Street at North Avenue
🚇 North Avenue (N3)
End point High Museum of Art
🚻 F3
✉ 1280 Peachtree Street
🚇 Arts Center (N5)

The Westin Peachtree Plaza Hotel

EVENING STROLLS

Most crimes in Atlanta take place at night, so on these evening strolls exercise extreme caution and stick to the route advised. If you suspect there may be danger, enter a hotel, store, or restaurant.

LITTLE FIVE POINTS

Little Five Points is Atlanta's version of New York City's Greenwich Village, a small bohemian quarter with interesting music clubs, restaurants, art galleries and theaters, and health-food stores, groceries, and offbeat shops. It is best seen at night when the clubs are open and its regulars—artists, aging hippies, grunge rockers, and other alternative-culture types—are here in full force. Beginning at Austin and Euclid Avenues, follow Euclid Avenue north to Moreland Avenue and a plaza area where street musicians, mimes, and other performers entertain pedestrians. A few more stores are found off the plaza on Moreland and Seminole Avenues. There are stores on both sides of the street, so repeat the route to avoid crossing back and forth.

DOWNTOWN

Downtown Atlanta is very pretty when lit up at night. From the Upper Alabama Street level at Underground Atlanta (➤ 29), go to its Central Avenue end and peer across the railing at the State Capitol of Georgia (➤ 27), The World of Coca-Cola (➤ 28) with its dramatic pinwheeling neon logo, and the fountain at Depot Plaza. Backtracking, pause to look at the skyscrapers northward, then follow Peachtree Street to Woodruff Park (➤ 59) for another view of the buildings. Half a mile farther on at International Boulevard, turn right down the hill to Courtland Street, turning around for another good view of the skyline. Continue left to Baker Street, then left back up to Peachtree Street, crossing to Hardy Ivy Park, then right on West Peachtree Street to the MARTA Civic Center station. Just beyond the station are good sight lines back up Peachtree and views of the skyscrapers in Midtown.

ORGANIZED SIGHTSEEING

AMERICAN SIGHTSEEING ATLANTA

Runs the following tours: "Atlanta…A City of Winners," which covers the city highlights; and "Homegrown Hits," which goes to CNN, The World of Coca-Cola, and Underground Atlanta. An all-day excursion to Stone Mountain Park includes a skylift trip to the top of the mountain and a cruise on a paddle-wheel riverboat.
✉ 550 Pharr Road ☎ 404/233–9140 or 800/572–3050

ATLANTA PRESERVATION CENTER

Volunteers lead ten inexpensive walking tours of historic areas and neighborhoods, including the Fox Theatre, Sweet Auburn/Martin Luther King, Jr. National Historic District, Druid Hills, Inman Park, Historic Downtown, Ansley Park, Piedmont Park, and Underground Atlanta.
✉ 156 7th Street ☎ 404/876–2041 or 404/876–2040

GRAY LINE OF ATLANTA

Provides short tours of Downtown, Midtown, and Buckhead, and a day-long tour that covers Atlanta's primary sights and attractions, plus Stone Mountain and the King Center.
✉ 2541 Camp Creek Parkway, College Park
☎ 404/767–0594

LOWDER CITY TOURS

Offers thematic tours of Atlanta's historic sites, Stone Mountain Park, Atlanta nightlife, black heritage, and a tour they call "Carter, King, and Coke" for all group sizes (limousine, van, or passenger bus). Tours are between three and eight hours in length.
✉ 131 Ponce de Leon Avenue ☎ 800/354–1961 or 404/874–1349

Bird's-eye view

Historic Air Tours (✉ DeKalb-Peachtree Airport, in the suburb of Chamblee ☎ 770/457–5217 for correct street entrance) takes visitors high above the city in a private, four-seater Cessna 172 airplane for a dramatic bird's-eye perspective of the city, focusing primarily on architectural and historic highlights. Its three tours range from 20 to 55 minutes long.

Midtown skyline from Piedmont Park Lake

EXCURSIONS

INFORMATION

Kennesaw Mountain National Battlefield Park

Distance 25 miles north of downtown Atlanta

Time 30–45 minutes

Directions Follow I-75 north to exit 116, Barrett Parkway. Turn left, then follow signs

🚩 Off map at C1

✉ 900 Kennesaw Mountain Drive, Kennesaw, GA 30144

☎ 770/427–4687

🕐 Daily 8:30–5

🎟 Free

Roswell

Distance 15 miles north of Buckhead

Time 30–45 minutes

Directions Follow Roswell Road (US 19) north from Peachtree Road in Buckhead to the town square, or take GA 400 north to the second Northridge Road exit (pass under bridge). Turn right to Roswell Road, then right again

🚩 Off map at F1

✉ 617 Atlanta Street, Roswell, GA 30075 (Historic Roswell Convention & Visitors Center)

☎ 770/640–3253

🕐 Mon–Fri 9–5; Sat 10–4; Sun 12–3

🚌 85 from Lenox station (N7)

🎟 Free for walking tour; inexpensive for Bulloch Hall

KENNESAW MOUNTAIN NATIONAL BATTLEFIELD PARK

Kennesaw Mountain, located a short distance northwest of Atlanta near Marietta, was an important military objective of the Union Army in 1864, one of the last major barriers before reaching Atlanta. The 2,882-acre park preserves the site of the crucial battle, which lasted from June 5 to July 2 and pitted 100,000 Union soldiers against 50,000 Confederates. Cannons, monuments, markers, earthworks, and a small museum tell the story of the battle. There are also 16 miles of hiking trails, with a couple of strenuous ascents up the mountain as a contrast to the surrounding flat and rolling terrain.

ROSWELL

The historic suburb of Roswell, located a few miles north of the Chattahoochee River, offers a look at the Old South. Founded in 1839, it managed to survive the onslaught of Sherman's Union Army, which destroyed only the mills that supplied cotton and woolen goods to the Confederate Army. The Roswell Historical Society provides a walking tour of 22 stately mansions and buildings from the 1840s, plus a river crossing, the original town square, and three cemeteries. Bulloch Hall (➤ 52) is the only home regularly open to the public.

Kennesaw Mountain National Battlefield Park

CHATEAU ÉLAN WINERY

Begun in 1981, Château Élan is Georgia's premier winery and a popular resort spread over 2,400 acres of rolling countryside. Within its main building, a replicated French château, there are tours of the winery with free samples, a wine market, gift shop, art gallery, bistro, and formal restaurant. The resort area includes two golf courses, a health spa, tennis center, equestrian center, and a conference center. Several annual events, including British Car Day (May) and Bastille Day (July 14), make it a fun place to visit.

Chateau Élan Winery

BRASSTOWN BALD

At 4,874 feet above sea level, Brasstown Bald is the highest point in Georgia, with a panoramic view of the southern Appalachian Mountains. The visitors center explains the mountain's history and has displays of native plants and wildlife. The mountains here are especially pretty in the spring when wildflowers bloom, and in the fall when tree foliage turns to brilliant shades of yellow, orange, and red. En route to this site, you will pass through Helen, a replica of a Bavarian alpine village, and cross the Appalachian Trail, a 2,000-mile hiking trail that runs from Georgia to Maine.

INFORMATION

Chateau Élan Winery

Distance 40 miles northeast of downtown Atlanta

Time 45–60 minutes

Directions Take I-85 north to exit 48 (GA 211); turn left and continue for a short distance

✚ Off map at G1

✉ 100 Tour de France, Braselton, GA 30075

☎ 800/847–6705; 770/271–6050

🕐 10–10

🎫 Free for winery; admission charge for some festivals

Brasstown Bald

Distance 115 miles north of downtown Atlanta

Time 2 hours

Directions Take I-85 north, diverging left on to I-985. Turn left at GA 52 and right at US 129 to Cleveland. Turn right at GA 75 to Helen and AT trail, left at GA 180, then right at GA 180 spur to Brasstown Bald parking lot

✚ Off map at G1

✉ Administrator: 1881 Highway 515, Blairsville, GA 30512

☎ Visitors center: 706/896–2555

🕐 Jun 1–Nov 15 daily 10–6. Apr–May Sat–Sun 10–6. Closed Nov 16–Mar 31

🎫 Parking fee

WHAT'S ON

Atlanta hosts numerous annual events. Those listed below and others are described in the *Atlanta Journal* and *Atlanta Constitution*'s Friday "Weekend Preview" or Saturday "Leisure" tabloid sections and several other publications (➤ 92).

JANUARY   *King Week*: remembers Martin Luther King, Jr. through a week-long festival of lectures, films, parades, and musical entertainment

APRIL   *Dogwood Festival*: a week-long celebration of spring, with concerts, home tours, craft shows, and a balloon race starting at Piedmont Park

Inman Park Festival and Tour of Homes: an excellent opportunity to explore the interiors of the Victorian homes in Atlanta's oldest suburb

JULY   *Independence Day*: begins with the annual Peachtree Road Race, followed by a parade, and culminates with gigantic firework displays

National Black Arts Festival: a week-long celebration of black culture through art exhibits, films, music, and literature

SEPTEMBER   *Arts Festival of Atlanta* (Sep 5–21): formerly held in Piedmont Park, and the annual event that Atlantans look forward to most; now being held in Centennial Olympic Park (➤ 59) and other Downtown venues. The outdoor event brings some of the best craftspeople, visual artists, theater and street performers to the city. The Artist's Market is the main draw, with theatrical and musical entertainment attracting large crowds at night

Yellow Daisy Festival: in Stone Mountain Park; features 400 arts and craftspeople, as well as entertainment

OCTOBER   *Scottish Festival and Highland Games*: in Stone Mountain Park; attracts over 100 clans for a celebration of dance, music, and traditional games

NOVEMBER   *Lighting of the Great Tree (Atlanta city Christmas tree)*: accompanied by choirs and musicians; held at Underground Atlanta

DECEMBER   *Macy's Eggleston Christmas Parade*: on Peachtree Street

Festival of Trees: displays over 200 Christmas trees decorated by local designers, garden clubs, and schools

ATLANTA
top 25 sights

The sights are shown on the inside front cover and inside back cover, numbered **1–25** from south to north across the city

1

ZOO ATLANTA

INFORMATION

- H9
- 800 Cherokee Avenue
- 404/624–5600
- During Daylight Saving Time (mid-spring–mid-fall) Mon–Fri 10–4:30; Sat–Sun 10–5:30. Rest of year daily 10–4:30. Closed Jan 1, 3rd Mon in Jan, 4th Thu in Nov, Dec 25
- Good café with southern-style meals ($$); several concession stands and snack bars ($)
- Five points (0), then Zoo Trolley (summer months), 31, 32, 97
- Very good
- Expensive
- Cyclorama (► 25), Oakland Cemetery (► 33)
- Guided group tours. Gift shops, lecture series, workshops, day camps for children, and numerous annual events including night walks and behind-the-scenes visits

Not so long ago the city zoo was a disgrace, a dirty facility with animals crammed into small and unsanitary cages. Now, however, it has been given a new lease of life through a hugely successful $35 million renovation program.

Wildlife education Zoo Atlanta's 40 acres are home to more than 1,000 animals which enjoy habitats that replicate those of their original geographical homes. Adjacent to each habitat are signs, exhibits, information stations, or video displays to educate visitors about the animal and its environment. Regular feedings and entertaining demonstrations offer further insight into the animals.

Lions, tigers, and more Not to be missed are the African habitats of Mzima Springs, an East African watering hole where you'll view several elephants; and Masai Mara, which simulates the expansive Kenya plains with roaming zebras, black rhinoceroses, gazelles, and ostriches. Lions overlook the scene from a rock-outcrop enclosure. Next door is the lush Ford African Rain Forest, a series of gorilla and monkey environments separated by moats. Among its residents is the zoo mascot Willie B, a male gorilla who hit the headlines when he finally fathered a child (Kudzu) after a decade of trying. Other highlights include Ketambe, a re-created Indonesian tropical rain forest with rare Sumatran tigers and orangutans; Sea Lion Cove, which features underwater viewing of sea lions; Flamingo Lagoon, with baby pink Chilean flamingos; the Reptile House, with exotic and slithery creatures from around the world; and the Children's Zoo, with an area where animals can be petted. Future wildlife exhibits include the Okefenokee Swamp/ Georgia Coast, with alligators and otters.

CYCLORAMA

On first view Cyclorama appears to be just a big painting. But that all changes as the narration begins. Almost immediately, you become sucked into the sound and fury of battle, with muskets roaring and the screaming of wounded soldiers.

Civil War drama unfolds The Battle of Atlanta, which took place on July 22, 1864, is vividly brought to life at Cyclorama. Here, a circular three-dimensional oil painting, 358 feet in circumference and 42 feet high, combines with *faux-terrain* dioramas extending 30 feet outward from the painting, plus special sound effects, lighting, music, and narration. The battle is viewed from a slowly revolving seat platform in the inner core of the painting. The 16,000-square foot canvas, painted on Belgian linen, was completed in 1886 by 11 Eastern European artists. Following damage over the years by bacteria, water, insects, rodents and other elements, an $11 million restoration program in the 1970s returned it to its original splendor.

Other attractions The building housing Cyclorama also contains a museum with Civil War artifacts, paintings, photographs, weapons, uniforms, maps, the steam locomotive *Texas*, and a video presentation about the restoration.

HIGHLIGHTS

- Cyclorama painting
- Dioramas
- Multimedia production
- "Life in Camp" display
- Cannons
- Weapons
- Uniforms
- Confederate leader portraits
- Union leader portraits
- Civil War photographs
- *Texas* steam locomotive

INFORMATION

- ✚ H8
- ✉ 800 Cherokee Avenue
- ☎ 404/658–7625. Recorded information: 404/624–1071
- 🕐 Oct–May daily 9:30–4:30. Jun–Sep daily 9:30–5:30. Closed Jan 1, 3rd Mon in Jan, 4th Thu in Nov, Dec 25
- 🚇 Five Points (0), then bus 31, 97; or King Memorial (E2), then bus 32
- ♿ Good
- 💰 Moderate
- ↔ Zoo Atlanta (➤ 24), Oakland Cemetery (➤ 33)
- ❓ Cyclorama show every half hour. Gift shop

Cyclorama houses the famous oil painting of the Battle of Atlanta

3

WREN'S NEST

HIGHLIGHTS

- Tar Baby doll
- Uncle Remus character sculptures
- Br'er Fox doll
- Carved-wood Br'er Rabbit tobacco-holder
- Life-size Uncle Remus diorama
- Japanese edition of *Uncle Remus*
- Harris's typewriter
- Original mailbox
- Gas-light fixtures
- "Grumble Box"

INFORMATION

- ✚ C8
- ✉ 1050 Ralph David Abernathy Boulevard
- ☎ 404/753–7735. Recorded information: 404/753–8535
- ◷ Tue–Sat 10–4; Sun 1–4. Closed Jan 1, 4th Thu in Nov, Dec 24–25
- Ⓟ West End (S2)
- 🚌 71
- ♿ None
- 💲 Moderate
- ❓ Atlanta Preservation "West End" walking tour (► 19). Storytelling every Sat; Wren's Nest Fest (May); Christmas Festival (Dec)

Many people will remember the captivating children's tales of Uncle Remus, *featuring Br'er Fox and Tar Baby. It's interesting to see where this author worked, his possessions providing clues to his era, and influences.*

An author's home The Wren's Nest, an 1870s farmhouse with a Queen Anne/Victorian façade, was the home of Georgia author and journalist Joel Chandler Harris (1848–1908), who wrote many of the *Uncle Remus* stories from a wicker rocking chair on the wraparound porch. Named after a family of wrens that once nested in the mailbox, the house has nine rooms filled with family memorabilia, furnishings and photographs, first-edition copies of the *Uncle Remus* tales in several foreign languages, and oddities such as the "Grumble Box," a small wooden box set on the dining-room table within which Chandler's daughters deposited a coin every time he or his wife caught them complaining.

Creating a classic A slide presentation shows how Chandler began his writing career at the age of 13 as an apprentice—for four years—on a plantation newspaper in central Georgia. It was there, listening to the slaves, that he became enchanted for a lifetime by their African folk tales of talking animals. In 1877, while employed as an editorial columnist for the *Atlanta Constitution*, he recalled these tales when thinking about a topic for his next column. With the goal to recapture their spirit, his stories feature a black narrator and the authentic slave dialects.

The tradition of storytelling To perpetuate Chandler's love of storytelling, members of the Southern Order of Storytellers narrate tales here every Saturday at 2PM.

4

STATE CAPITOL OF GEORGIA

A visit to the State Capitol when the state legislature is in session is especially interesting and entertaining. With a number of flamboyant characters and a helter skelter atmosphere, these sessions often resemble a three-ring circus.

Exterior The neoclassical-styled Georgia State Capitol building, dedicated on July 4, 1889, was Atlanta's first symbol of rebirth from the Civil War. Its shiny, 75-foot-high gold dome, topped by a statue of Liberty, is a city landmark visible from several downtown locations. The double-winged building features a majestic entrance: a four-story portico with stairs leading up to the second level, its upper pediment supported by six, two-story-tall Corinthian columns. In the grounds, shaded by large oak and magnolia trees, are state historical markers commemorating the Battle of Atlanta and various statues representing famous Georgians.

Interior The marbled 237-foot-high rotunda is filled with marble busts and portraits of past governors, plus tattered flags from Georgia Civil War regiments. Hanging from the staircases leading to the legislative chambers in both wings are flags from all 50 states as well as those that have flown over Georgia, including a British flag and several of the Confederacy. On the fourth floor is the Georgia State Museum of Science and Industry (➤ 54).

The Hall of Flags

HIGHLIGHTS

- Gold dome
- Main entrance
- Rotunda
- Hall of Flags south wing
- Hall of Flags north wing
- Confederate regiment flags
- Military rifle collection (museum)
- Native American exhibit (museum)
- Two-headed cow (museum)

INFORMATION

- ➕ F7
- ✉ 206 Washington Street
- ☎ 404/656–2000
- 🎦 State Capitol: free guided tours Mon–Fri 10AM, 11AM, 1PM and 2PM.
  Georgia State Museum of Science and Industry: Mon–Fri 8–5; Sat 10–4; Sun noon–4. Closed Jan 1, Easter Mon, last Mon in May, Jul 4, 1st Mon in Sep, 4th Thu in Nov, Dec 24–25
- 🍴 Good cafeteria ($) in building opposite, part of Georgia State station
- 🚇 Georgia State (E1)
- 🚌 9, 10, 21, 55, 74, 90, 97
- ♿ Good
- 💲 Free
- ↔ The World of Coca-Cola (➤ 28), Underground Atlanta (➤ 29), Atlanta Heritage Row (➤ 30)
- ❓ Indian Heritage Week (2nd week in Nov)

27

THE WORLD OF COCA-COLA

HIGHLIGHTS

- Revolving entrance sign
- Bottling fantasy sculpture
- 1930s soda fountain
- Club Coca-Cola
- Copy of original formula
- Vintage magazine advertisements
- Classic television commercials
- Radio jingles on a 1930s jukebox
- Antique bottling equipment
- Coca-Cola toys

INFORMATION

- ✚ F7
- ✉ 55 Martin Luther King, Jr. Drive
- ☎ Recorded information/voice mail: 404/676–5151
- ◷ Mon–Sat 10–9:30; Sun noon–6. Closed Jan 1, 2nd Mon in Jan, Easter Mon, 4th Thu in Nov, Dec 24–25
- 🍴 Coca-Cola product drinks only (free); several restaurants and fast-food outlets at nearby Underground Atlanta
- 🚇 Georgia State (E1), Five Points (0)
- 🚌 4, 9, 10, 17, 49, 74, 90, 97
- ♿ Very good
- 💲 Inexpensive
- ↔ State Capitol of Georgia (➤ 27), Underground Atlanta (➤ 29), Atlanta Heritage Row (➤ 30)
- ❓ Gift shop

Although this museum is just one big advertisement for Coca-Cola—hardly necessary for the world's most popular soft drink—it is worth seeing for its high-tech exhibits and to drink samples of Coca-Cola products sold in other countries.

Atlanta's finest company The World of Coca-Cola presents the drink—served for the first time in 1886 at an Atlanta pharmacy soda fountain—plus its history and projections for the future. After passing beneath a revolving Coca-Cola globe hanging 18 feet above the entrance—a special sight at night with its flashing, pinwheel pattern—you enter a three-story atrium connected to four gallery exhibit areas.

Celebrating a product Gallery One features a futuristic look at the bottling process through a whimsical, kinetic sculpture and over 1,000 pieces of memorabilia from company archives. In the second gallery is a replica 1930s soda fountain, while in the third gallery a high-tech film takes a look at the product's international character. The final gallery shows the drink's

advertising history, including infamous jingles such as "Coke is It." Before leaving, stop at Club Coca-Cola, a futuristic soda fountain where you can sip samples of the Coca-Cola products; and at the Trademart gift shop, which is full of clothing and many souvenirs bearing the Coca-Cola logo.

6

UNDERGROUND ATLANTA

Beneath Peachtree Street is essentially another city, one that actually existed in the past. The sound of trains passing on the nearby tracks makes it easy to imagine what the early days of Atlanta might have been like.

On historical ground Underground Atlanta—located a few steps southwest of the point where Atlanta began as a railroad terminus in 1837—is a unique juxtaposition of past history and modern elements. Spanning an extensive area covering six blocks, this entertainment and shopping complex was created by restoring the underground brick streets, ornamental building façades, and tunnels that had fallen into disuse in 1929 after the city authorities built viaducts over the railroad tracks in order to accommodate motorized traffic.

Shopping and sights Underground Atlanta's Upper and Lower Alabama Streets feature specialty stores selling art, books, clothes, regional foods, and souvenirs from the original storefronts. Adding to the constant festival-like atmosphere are street performers and some 50 merchants hawking a variety of goods from pushcarts. Also here are the Olympic Experience, an audio-visual presentation and information center about the Olympic Games held in Atlanta in 1996; Atlanta Heritage Row; and Peachtree Fountains Plaza, which fronts the main entrance with a series of cascading waterfalls and fountains.

Nightlife At the lowest level of Underground Atlanta is Kenny's Alley, with bars and nightspots that offer various comedy acts, music, and dancing. The alley itself was once occupied by saloons and livery stables.

HIGHLIGHTS

- Atlanta Heritage Row
- Olympic Experience
- Peachtree Fountains Plaza
- Kenny's Alley
- Historic building façades
- Pushcart merchants
- Upper Alabama shops
- Lower Alabama shops
- Wall murals
- Live alligators at Dante's Down the Hatch nightclub (➤ 81)

INFORMATION

- ✚ F7
- ✉ Between Peachtree Street and Central Avenue at Upper Alabama Street
- ☎ 404/523–2311
- 🕐 Retail shops: Mon–Sat 10–9:30; Sun noon–6. Restaurants and Kenny's Alley: midnight–2AM
- 🍽 Restaurants ($$–$$$); food court with some 20 fast-food vendors ($)
- 🚇 Five Points (0)
- 🚌 3, 4, 9, 13, 17, 20, 31, 42, 49, 90, 97
- ♿ Good (call in advance for directions to elevators)
- 🎟 Free to browse
- ↔ Atlanta Heritage Row (➤ 30), The World of Coca-Cola (➤ 28)
- ❓ Atlanta Preservation walking tour (➤ 19). "Lighting of the Great Tree" (city Christmas tree ➤ 22); New Year's Eve celebration

ATLANTA HERITAGE ROW

HIGHLIGHTS

- Early Native American display
- Re-created railway station
- Battle of Atlanta bomb shelter
- Grady's New South speech
- 1920s trolley car
- Martin Luther King, Jr.'s pulpit
- *Gone with the Wind* première video
- Blues and country music
- *People: The Spirit of Atlanta* video
- Delta jet cockpit

INFORMATION

- ✚ F7
- ✉ 55 Upper Alabama Street at Underground Atlanta
- ☎ 404/584–7879
- ◷ Tue–Sat 10–5; Sun 1–5. Closed Jan 1, 4th Thu in Nov, Dec 25
- 🍴 Fast-food court and restaurants at Underground Atlanta (➤ 29)
- 🚇 Five Points (0)
- 🚌 3, 4, 9, 13, 17, 20, 31, 42, 49, 90, 97
- ♿ Very good
- ✋ Inexpensive
- ↔ State Capitol of Georgia (➤ 27), The World of Coca-Cola (➤ 28), Underground Atlanta (➤ 29)
- ❓ Occasional special events

Most history museums, with their undistinguished rows of display cases, can be boring. It's a shame they are not like Atlanta Heritage Row, where you are thrust into the middle of a re-created event. Witnessing it up close makes history come alive—and for a moment you become part of it.

Reliving history Atlanta Heritage Row is a fascinating multimedia presentation that makes Atlanta's history come alive by putting the viewer directly in the middle of the action. The show is divided into six historical periods, with each section of touchable, lifelike exhibits merging into the next with the aid of sound, videos, and a time line. When you pass out of Origins (early Native Americans–1860) into the Civil War (1861–1865), you enter a Battle of Atlanta bomb shelter amid rubble and the sounds of cannon fire, backed by narration from the diaries of those who lived during the time.

Historical eras Other themes include Atlanta Resurgens (1865–1895), with journalist Henry Grady's infamous speech advancing his ideas for a New South; Forward Atlanta (1895–1945), with a 1920s trolley car; and Big League City (1945–1974), where you can stand at Martin Luther King, Jr.'s pulpit to experience his famous "I Have a Dream" speech.

International City International City (1974–present) brings the story of Atlanta up to date. Here you can enter the cockpit of a 1970s Delta Airline jet plane and listen to communications with the control tower. The self-guided tour ends with a 15-minute, high-tech, wide-screen video called *People: The Spirit of Atlanta*.

CNN CENTER

It's easy to flip on the television and watch the news, but you'll never take it for granted again after visiting the CNN studio. To see the steps taken (amid chaos) to get the news to the viewers is enlightening.

Ted Turner's world CNN Center is the headquarters of the internationally broadcasted Cable News Network and Headline News, two 24-hour all news networks. A 45-minute studio tour begins by riding up the world's longest escalator to an eighth-floor exhibit on Turner's global broadcasting empire. This includes MGM movie stills, a Galaxy 5 satellite replica, exhibits about the Jacques Cousteau and National Geographic programs carried on the TBS cable station, and items from CNN's 1990–1991 Gulf War reportage.

The CNN studio From here you get to witness news in the making as reporters scurry to finish stories—while overhead banks of monitors show the latest events breaking from around the world. Editors and producers coordinate the stories as on-the-air personalities prepare to deliver the news.

HIGHLIGHTS

- CNN news room
- MGM movie stills
- Galaxy 5 satellite replica
- TBS sports exhibit
- Jacques Cousteau exhibit
- National Geographic exhibit
- Gulf War reportage exhibit
- *Gone with the Wind* Oscar replica
- The Turner Store
- World's longest escalator

INFORMATION

- ✚ F6
- ✉ 1 CNN Center, Marietta Street
- ☎ 404/827–1500. Recorded information: 404/827–2300
- 🕐 Daily 9–5. Closed Jan 1, Easter Mon, last Mon in May, Jul 4, 1st Mon in Sep, 4th Thu in Nov, Dec 24–25
- 🍴 Several restaurants ($$) and fast-food outlets ($)
- 🚇 Omni/Dome/GWCC (W1)
- 🚌 1, 11, 18, 86
- ♿ Excellent
- ✋ Moderate
- ↔ Omni Coliseum, Georgia World Congress Center and Georgia Dome are next door
- ❓ Visits by guided tour only. Reservations are strongly recommended. Not suitable for children under 6

The world's longest escalator

SWEET AUBURN

HIGHLIGHTS

- Tomb
- MLK Center museum
- King's birthplace, 501 Auburn Avenue
- Fire Station 6 (c. 1894), Auburn Avenue at Boulevard
- Ebenezer Baptist Church (c. 1894), 407 Auburn Avenue
- African-American Panoramic Experience Museum, 135 Auburn Avenue
- Big Bethel African Methodist Episcopal Church (c. 1891), 220 Auburn Avenue

INFORMATION

Avoid at night
- ✚ G6–H6
- ✉ Auburn Avenue from Courtland Street to Howell Street. MLK Center: 449 Auburn Avenue
- ☎ 404/524–1956
- ⏰ Summer daily 9–8. Rest of year daily 9–5:30. Closed Dec 25
- 🍴 Snack area in MLK Center; a few restaurants ($–$$) on Auburn Avenue
- Ⓖ King Memorial (E2)
- 🚌 3, 17, 99
- ♿ Good
- Ⓖ Inexpensive
- ↔ Oakland Cemetery (➤ 33)
- ❓ Daily tours begin at 9:30AM. Atlanta Preservation walking tour (➤ 19). King Week (2nd week in Jan). At MLK Center: gift shop, conferences and ongoing lecture series

Considering how race relations have improved in Atlanta in the past two decades, it's hard to imagine that this area was once run solely by blacks and that they were excluded from the white business community just a few blocks away.

Sweet Auburn The influence of African-Americans—who comprise more than 60 percent of Atlanta's population—has been felt most along Auburn Avenue. This district is connected to Downtown, and from 1890 to 1930 was the most prosperous center of black business, entertainment, and political life. Prevented from participating in the white business community, black Atlantans came here to open businesses, attend church and fraternal organizations, and to party.

Martin Luther King, Jr. National Historic District This is located at Sweet Auburn's eastern end, and was established by the National Park Service in 1980 to preserve the birthplace and boyhood surroundings of the nation's most renowned Civil Rights leader. In the courtyard of the Martin Luther King, Jr. Center for Non-Violent Social Change is King's raised white marble tomb, set in the middle of a "meditation"

pool and with the inscription "Free at last." The center's museum contains King's Nobel Peace Prize, Bible, typewriter, and many photographs that chronicle the Civil Rights movement.

The birthplace of Martin Luther King, Jr.

OAKLAND CEMETERY

This cemetery is reminiscent of many in Europe—not just a burial plot, but a treasure trove of art and history. Along its hilly paths, shaded by massive oak trees, are elaborately decorated burial markers, monuments, and fountains.

A Who's Who of deceased Atlantans Oakland Cemetery, the city's oldest burial ground, contains a mixed assortment of Atlanta citizens. It opened in 1850 and was the only municipal cemetery in Atlanta until 1884. Among its 100,000 occupants are rich and poor, black and white, Christian and Jew, and a host of celebrities, including the modest graves of *Gone with the Wind* author Margaret Mitchell (Marsh), Inman Park developer Joel Hurt (▶ 34), and famed 1930s golfer Bobby Jones, plus 23 Atlanta mayors, six Georgia governors, and five Confederate generals.

Graveyard art Listed on the National Register of Historic Places, the still-used 88-acre cemetery has an incredible collection of Gothic and Classic Revival mausoleums decorated with beautiful stained glass, flamboyant Gothic accents, and sculpture. Made from cast iron, bronze, or stone, the tombs are exquisite examples of artistic craftsmanship, often depicting symbolic Christian metaphors such as crosses, swords, lions, and angels.

Battle of Atlanta section From Oakland's highest hill, Confederate Commander-in-Chief General John B. Hood surveyed his troops during the Battle of Atlanta. The Confederate Army section, marked by a striking monument of a wounded lion, contains nearly 3,000 soldiers buried here by women and children shortly after the battle.

HIGHLIGHTS

- Jasper Newton Smith statue/mausoleum
- Austell mausoleum
- Marion Kiser mausoleum
- E. W. Marsh mausoleum
- Konz family "Egyptian-style" monument
- "Weeping Woman" statue
- Maurine Robbins tomb
- Neal family monument
- William Allen Fuller monument
- "Children Out in the Rain" fountain

INFORMATION

Avoid at night

- G/H7
- ✉ 248 Oakland Avenue
- ☎ 404/688–2107
- 🕐 Daily 8–6
- 🚇 King Memorial (E2)
- 🚌 9, 18, 32
- ♿ None
- 🎟 Free; walking-tour brochure available at cemetery office (modest price)
- ↔ Zoo Atlanta (▶ 24), Cyclorama (▶ 25), MLK Center for Non-Violent Social Change (▶ 32)
- ❓ Tours for groups of 10–30 by appointment: May–Oct Sat 11; Sun 2. Annual "Sunday in the Park" festival (Oct)

INMAN PARK

INFORMATION

The 19th-century Victorian homes of Inman Park are not to be viewed in a hurry. You may find yourself staring at a house, closely examining every turret, fish scale shingle, gable, balcony, fancy molding, and ornate feature.

Atlanta's first suburb Developed in the 1880s by Joel Hurt, the Inman Park neighborhood—located east of downtown Atlanta near the site of a crucial Civil War battle—was Atlanta's first suburb. Connected to the commercial district by one of the nation's first electric streetcar systems, it swiftly became Atlanta's most prestigious address, attracting such luminaries as Coca-Cola founder Asa G. Candler, who owned Callan Castle, a huge Greek Revival-style mansion. Hurt owned two homes here, a modest cottage and a large half-Italianate, half-Victorian-styled mansion. He named the neighborhood after his friend Samuel M. Inman.

20th-century changes By 1910, Inman Park began losing residents to newer developed 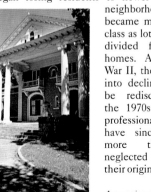 neighborhoods and became more middle class as lots were subdivided for smaller homes. After World War II, the area went into decline, only to be rediscovered in the 1970s by young professionals who have since restored more than 100 neglected homes to their original splendor.

A mansion on Inman Park

CARTER PRESIDENTIAL CENTER & LIBRARY

Washington, D.C., may be home to the White House, but this Center offers a better chance to get a close look at the life of a President. Through high-tech interactive videos, you can even talk to President Carter about issues in his administration.

The Carter Presidential Center and Library is located on historic Copenhill. At this vantage point—which overlooks downtown Atlanta—General Sherman watched the raging battle from the Augustus Hurt House.

Understated exterior The Center consists of four austere, circular buildings. The approach leads along a winding driveway, lined with flags from many nations, to a central fountained pool and double-colonnaded entrance. Behind the Center is a Japanese garden, with beautiful flowers, shrubbery, and a man-made stream, lake, and waterfall. This is a serene spot in which to relax, and offers views of the Atlanta skyline.

Carter Library Museum The exhibits in the Carter Library Museum use documents, furniture, clothes, and family mementos to celebrate Jimmy Carter's life from his early days as a peanut farmer in central Georgia to his roles as naval officer, state senator, Georgia governor, U.S. President, and humanitarian. Planned as a complete learning facility, the museum also examines the presidency in general, with a film and temporary exhibits that portray various historical aspects of the position. The Center's library, for use by appointment, can be viewed from the museum through a glass partition. It contains over 27 million pages of documents, 1.5 million photographs, and hours of audio- and videotapes.

HIGHLIGHTS

- Re-created Oval Office
- Carter's early years exhibit
- Presidential issues exhibit
- Japanese garden
- Gifts from foreign leaders
- Town Meeting exhibit
- 1976 presidential campaign memorabilia
- Presidential history film
- State dinner table setting replica
- Interactive "Carter" videos

INFORMATION

- ➕ J5
- ✉ 1 Copenhill Avenue
- ☎ 404/331–3942. Recorded information: 404/331–0296
- 🕐 Mon–Sat 9–4:45; Sun noon–4:45. Closed Jan 1, 4th Thu in Nov, Dec 25
- 🍴 Good cafeteria ($; Mon–Sat 11–4; Sun noon–4:30)
- Ⓜ Inman Park–Reynoldstown (E3)
- 🚌 2, 16
- ♿ Very good
- 💲 Moderate; children under 16 free
- ↔ Inman Park (➤ 34), Little Five Points (➤ 18)
- ❓ Group tours. Temporary art and history exhibits. Conferences by invitation only

13

FERNBANK MUSEUM OF NATURAL HISTORY

HIGHLIGHTS

- IMAX Theater
- *A Walk Through Time in Georgia*
- Dinosaur Hall
- Okefenokee Swamp exhibit
- Spectrum of the Senses
- The World of Shells
- Living Coral Reef & Tropical Fish Aquarium
- DNA model
- Rose gardens (outside)
- Fossil floor

INFORMATION

➕ Off map at K4

✉ 767 Clifton Road

☎ 404/378–0127. Recorded information: 404/370–0960. IMAX shows: 404/370–0019. Directions hot line: 404/370–0850

🕐 Mon–Thu, Sat 10–5; Fri 10–9; Sun noon–5. Closed Dec 25

🍴 Good dining room with light meals and snacks ($)

🚈 North Avenue (N3), then bus 2

♿ Museum: good. IMAX: call for special arrangements

✋ Museum or IMAX only: moderate. "Combination" ticket: very expensive

↔ Fernbank Science Center (➤ 37), Michael C. Carlos Museum (➤ 48)

❓ Gift shop, occasional workshops, lectures

While you are here, splurge on a film at the museum's IMAX Theater. It's an overwhelming experience, seeing things presented larger than life on the 52-foot by 70-foot screen—whether it's a national park or the Rolling Stones rock band.

The best in the South The Fernbank Museum maintains the largest natural history collection south of the Smithsonian Institution. Set within the 65-acre Fernbank Forest, this modern building—with a soaring 85-foot-high entrance atrium and fossils embedded into its limestone floor—features over 150,000 square feet of exhibition space that uses hands-on exhibits, interactive videos, and modern technology to explain the universe.

Popular exhibits Its most popular permanent exhibit, *A Walk Through Time in Georgia*, divides the state into six landform regions to explain how it developed over time. Utilizing large murals and dioramas, its best exhibits are Dinosaur Hall, with seven life-size creatures; and the Okefenokee Swamp, which re-creates the sights and sounds of this mysterious wet-

land. Other exhibits include the Spectrum of the Senses, The World of Shells, a decorative arts collection, and two hands-on Discovery Rooms for children. Fernbank also hosts some of the best exhibitions in North America.

A dinosaur skeleton found in the Gobi Desert, China

FERNBANK SCIENCE CENTER

On clear nights when specific planets or other celestial bodies are visible, Atlantans head for the Science Center Observatory, where the public is allowed to look at them up close through its 36-inch reflecting telescope.

Education and entertainment The Fernbank Science Center is the only museum in the United States owned and operated by a county school system. This small museum offers entertaining and educational exhibits focussing on ecology, geology, wildlife, space exploration, and modern technology. It has a meteor exhibit, the largest collection of Georgia tektites in the world, an authentic Apollo command module space capsule, a taxidermy reconstruction of a saber-toothed tiger, dioramas of insects, a vanishing wildlife habitats exhibit, and a rock and precious stone collection. As the predecessor of the newer and more elaborate Fernbank Museum of Natural History (➤ 36), there is some overlap of subject matter, including Okefenokee Swamp and dinosaur exhibits.

Planetarium Seating 500 people, the center's planetarium is the largest in the southeast United States. With a 70-foot projection dome, it features an amazing show of more than 9,000 stars and planets.

Nature trail The 2-mile paved nature trail through the adjoining Fernbank Forest offers peace and calm amid the bustle of the busy city as no recreational activities or picnics are allowed here. Fernbank Forest is an area of virgin woodland preserved by Emily Harrison, whose father, Colonel Z. Harrison, bought the land in 1881.

HIGHLIGHTS

- Observatory telescope
- Planetarium
- Okefenokee Swamp exhibit
- Dinosaurs
- Apollo space capsule
- Saber-toothed tiger
- Insect exhibits
- Rock and precious stone collection
- Fernbank Forest nature trails
- Georgia tektites collection

INFORMATION

- ✚ Off map at K4
- ✉ 156 Heaton Park Drive
- ☎ 404/378–4311. Recorded information: 404/378–4314
- 🕐 Mon 8:30–5; Tue–Fri 8:30–10; Sat 10–5; Sun 1–5. Extended vacation closings coincide with school system; call in advance
- 🚇 North Avenue (N3), then bus 2; or Edgewood–Candler Park (E4), then bus 12
- ♿ Good
- 🎟 Museum: free. Planetarium: inexpensive
- ↔ Fernbank Museum of Natural History (➤ 36), Michael C. Carlos Museum (➤ 48)
- ❓ Gift shop, workshops, lectures, films, open houses, and planetarium showings. Laboratory tours during open houses

15

STONE MOUNTAIN PARK

HIGHLIGHTS

- Top of Stone Mountain
- Confederate Memorial
- *Ante bellum* plantation
- Stone Mountain Scenic Railroad
- Paddle-wheel riverboat cruise
- Grist mill
- Antique cars
- Confederate Hall
- Recreational activities
- Laser light show

INFORMATION

- Off map at F4
- East on US 78 (look for exit signs)
- 770/498–5600
- Daily 6–midnight. Closed Dec 25
- Several restaurants ($$) and food concessions ($) throughout the park
- Avondale (E7), then bus 120
- Good at most attractions
- Park entrance fee (per car): moderate. Combination attractions ticket: expensive
- Regular festivals

On a clear day, the best view of the Atlanta metropolitan area is seen from atop Stone Mountain, an observation post used in past centuries by Native Americans, surveyors, and Civil War troops. Perhaps they too were awestruck by the view, especially the spectacular sunsets.

Stone Mountain Park, Georgia's number one tourist attraction, offers a cornucopia of things to see and do.

Confederate Memorial carving A prominent landmark visible from many Atlanta locations, Stone Mountain is the world's largest exposed granite outcrop (825 feet high). It is even more famous for the Confederate Memorial bas-relief sculpture carved into its rock face, a 90-foot-high by 190-foot-wide likeness of Confederate leaders Jefferson Davis, Robert E. Lee, and Stonewall Jackson on their horses.

Laser light show From April to November, the lawn beneath the sculpture is packed every night with people watching the spectacular laser light show cast on the mountain face. The top of the mountain can be reached by following a 1¼-mile trail or by skylift.

Other attractions A combined historical display and recreational site, the 3,200-acre park also contains a reassembled, 19-building *ante bellum* plantation brought here from other Georgia locations; a steam locomotive ride around the mountain's 5-mile-diameter base; an antique auto and musical instruments museum; Civil War exhibits; and two golf courses, a beach, lake, zoo, campground, and paddle-wheel riverboat.

SCITREK

If you hate museums where it is just look and don't touch, visit SciTrek, where the exhibits require hands-on participation. It's a great place for the curious of all ages, and manages to turn the understanding of scientific principles into a fun activity.

Hands-on museum SciTrek, rated one of the top ten physical science museums in the United States, has more than 100 exhibits illustrating scientific principles through technology. In the Mechanics and Simple Machines exhibition hall, you can lift a real car engine with a basic pulley and gear system, or use a Bernoulli blower to suspend a ball in the air, plus there's a 44-foot-high Eiffel Tower replica made from 18,762 metal "Erector" set pieces. In the Light and Perception section you can become a human kaleidoscope, or freeze your shadow on a wall covered with light-sensitive film. The highlight of the Electricity and Magnetism exhibition is a Van de Graaf generator, which makes your hair stand on end by producing high-voltage static electricity. In Mathematica, the achievements of mathematicians from the 12th century to the present day are illustrated on a wall, and various exhibits demonstrate the laws of math.

Traveling shows and young children A fifth exhibition hall is reserved for traveling technology shows such as electric cars. The Kidspace section is for children aged 2–7, and teaches them the basic principles of science through play.

HIGHLIGHTS

- Plasma Walk
- Eiffel Tower replica
- Distortion room
- Van de Graaf generator
- Frozen shadow room
- Human gyroscope
- Benham's "color" disk
- Light Island
- Bernoulli blower
- *Impact!* gamelike video

INFORMATION

- ⊞ G5
- ⊠ 395 Piedmont Avenue
- ☎ Recorded information/voice mail: 404/522–5500
- ◷ Mon–Sat 10–5; Sun noon–5. Closed Jan 1, Easter Mon, 4th Thu in Nov, Dec 25
- 🍴 Small food concession
- Ⓟ Civic Center (N2)
- 🚌 16, 31, 46
- ♿ Very good
- 💲 Expensive
- ⟷ Atlanta Museum (➤ 40)
- ❓ Temporary exhibit tours. Gift shop, summer film festival, workshops, and family programs in conjunction with temporary exhibitions

An electrical demonstration with a Jacob's ladder

17

ATLANTA MUSEUM

HIGHLIGHTS

- Civil War rifles
- Japanese Zero airplane
- Napoleon's hair
- World War I cannon
- Davy Crockett's rifle
- Adolf Hitler's cigar box
- General Custer's hairbrush
- Queen Victoria's shawl
- Margaret Mitchell's armchair
- President Franklin D. Roosevelt's urinary jar

INFORMATION

- ✚ F5
- ✉ 537 Peachtree Street
- ☎ 404/872–8233
- ◐ By appointment only
- 🍴 Two excellent restaurants ($$) a half block north
- 🚇 North Avenue (N3)
- 🚌 2, 10, 27, 31
- ♿ None
- 💷 Inexpensive
- ↔ SciTrek (➤ 39), Fox Theatre (➤ 41), Road to Tara Museum (➤ 42)
- ❓ Antiques shop on first floor

This is the oddest museum in Atlanta, a hoarder's paradise that's both interesting and weird. A visit here is more like browsing through the attic of an eccentric old relative who collected anything that took his or her fancy.

History of a collector The Atlanta Museum, housed on the second floor of a 25-room, red-brick Victorian-style house built in 1900 for wealthy distillery owner Rufus M. Rose, founder of the Four Roses Distillery, is the private collection of J. H. Elliott. It contains an eclectic assortment of over 2,500 historical objects, most of which have nothing to do with Atlanta. Beginning his collection as a teenager in 1899 with Indian artifacts, Elliott moved into full gear when he entered the antiques trade in 1923. Eventually he ran out of room for his business and collection and moved into the Rufus Rose House in 1945. His antiques shop, now managed by his son and grandson, still occupies the first floor of the house.

An eclectic collection Although there are designated Margaret Mitchell and Civil War rooms (the latter has an especially good collection of weapons and uniform accessories), the collection's jumbled arrangement defies good organization. A case holding a stone and vase from Tutankhamun's tomb sits beside a lock of Napoleon's hair and a tablecloth belonging to Lafayette. Look for Adolf Hitler's cigar box, General Custer's hairbrush, Davy Crockett's rifle, and Queen Victoria's shawl. From a World War I cannon to a Japanese Zero airplane, there's so much crammed into this museum that you have to circle through its rooms more than once to make sure you've seen everything.

FOX THEATRE

You will never tire of the Fox Theatre, nor will it cease to amaze you. Like a madcap dream turned into reality, its interior and exterior are truly works of art. Before a show, arrive early so you can investigate every nook and cranny.

History preserved The glamorous Fox Theatre, still used for Broadway shows, rock concerts, dance performances, and film festivals, is one of only a few classic movie palaces left in the United States. It was built in 1929 in a fabulous Moorish-Egyptian style as the headquarters of Atlanta's Arabic Order of the Nobles of the Mystic Shrine (a Masonic order). When they ran into financial difficulty, it was purchased by movie mogul William Fox, who turned it into a theater. In 1978, facing destruction from the corporation who bought it, it was saved from the wrecking ball by a local preservation group.

Architecturally unique With walls of alternating cream- and buff-colored brick, its exterior features three copper-clad onion domes, watch towers, lancet arches, machicolated walls, and a huge bronze marquee over the entrance. Once inside the 4,518-seat auditorium, look upward at the mystical "sky" ceiling, complete with softly floating clouds and twinkling stars, which can be transformed into a morning or evening setting. The minarets and castellated walls make it feel like the courtyard of an Arabian palace.

HIGHLIGHTS

- Sky ceiling
- Marquee at night
- Moorish-designed side entrance
- Egyptian ballroom
- Brass-trimmed ticket booths
- Möller organ (3,622 pipes)
- Dress-circle promenade
- Men's and women's lounges
- Terrazzo-tile floors
- Sequined stage curtain design

INFORMATION

- F4
- 660 Peachtree Street
- 404/881–2100
- Determined by event
- Concession stand during events; good restaurant next door and opposite ($$)
- North Avenue (N3)
- 2, 10, 13, 27, 31, 45, 99
- Good
- Tours: expensive
- Atlanta Museum (➤ 40), Road to Tara Museum (➤ 42)
- Atlanta Preservation Walking tour (➤ 19)

19

ROAD TO TARA MUSEUM

HIGHLIGHTS

- Film clips
- Original posters
- Costume Gallery
- Movie props
- Autographed *Gone with the Wind* first editions
- Actor/actress photographs
- Doll Gallery
- Civil War exhibit
- Original costume sketches
- Foreign *Gone with the Wind* editions

INFORMATION

- F4
- 659 Peachtree Street
- 404/897–1939
- Mon–Sat 10–6; Sun 1–6. Closed Dec 25
- Good restaurants next door and opposite ($$)
- North Avenue (N3)
- 2, 10, 13, 27, 31, 45, 99
- Good
- Tours: moderate
- Atlanta Museum (➤ 40), Fox Theatre (➤ 41)
- Tours by prearranged appointment. Gift shop, occasional lectures, seminars

Visitors to Atlanta often ask where Tara, the ante bellum *mansion from* **Gone with the Wind**, *is located. Unfortunately, it doesn't exist. The only place to re-live that romantic tale is here, at the Road to Tara Museum.*

Truth and fiction The Road to Tara Museum, named after Margaret Mitchell's original title for the famed novel, houses an impressive collection of *Gone with the Wind* memorabilia that allows visitors to rediscover the Civil War from both real and fictional viewpoints. It also offers an in-depth look at Margaret Mitchell's life with film clips, personal letters, and photographs.

A classic movie Views of the movie, from its making to the completed product, are presented in three galleries. The main gallery has original posters, murals, and photographs to re-acquaint you with the movie's characters; the Costume Gallery has reproductions of the clothes worn by the cast; and the Doll Gallery features over 100 different *Gone with the Wind* character dolls created from 1937 to 1992. A film on the making of the movie is shown in the David O. Selznick Screening Room.

Historic location The former luxury Georgian Terrace Hotel, in which the museum is housed, was the place where Margaret Mitchell first presented her completed manuscript to her publisher, and also where the cast stayed for the 1939 Atlanta premiere.

Some members of the movie cast

HIGH MUSEUM OF ART

The High Museum is a sight to behold, both inside and out. Its bright white walls and vast sky-lit atrium create a light and airy atmosphere that makes it seem more like a garden than a museum, and ensures a pleasurable environment in which to view art.

Post-modern architecture The High Museum of Art, its exterior walls covered with white porcelain-enameled steel panels, is an innovative building that receives more raves for its architecture than its art collection. Built in 1983 by premier American architect Richard Meier, it resembles a giant cubist-geometric sculpture dropped on the lawn. From the pavement, a slanted entrance ramp leads upward to a three-story, bowed glass window that looks into a sky-lit atrium. A grand-piano-shaped lobby to the right juts outward, while a blocky, semi-detached auditorium building set at a 45-degree angle to the left completes the building's look from the street. Inside, galleries on all levels radiate in a semi-circular manner off the atrium.

Permanent collection The High Museum excels in American decorative arts, sub-Saharan African art, 19th-century American landscapes, American post-World War II modern works, and its Uhry Print Collection, which contains works by notable French Impressionists, Post-Impressionists, German Expressionists, and post-war American modern artists. It also has the obligatory Rodin sculpture and a large Alexander Calder mobile graces the front lawn.

Temporary exhibits These feature major artists, and are held at the museum every month.

HIGHLIGHTS

- *Houses of Parliament,* Claude Monet
- *Marilyn,* Andy Warhol
- *Beach at Sainte-Adresse,* Frédéric Bazille
- *Supreme Hardware Store,* Richard Estes
- *Pow!,* Roy Lichtenstein
- *Hayrick,* John Henry Twachtman
- *Descent Into Hell,* Albrecht Dürer
- *Venus,* Vincenzo Catena

INFORMATION

- ✠ F3
- ✉ 1280 Peachtree Street
- ☎ 404/733–4400. Recorded information: 404/733–HIGH
- 🕐 Tue–Thu 10–5; Fri 10–9; Sat 10–5; Sun noon–5. Closed Jan 1, Easter Mon, last Mon in May, Jul 4, 1st Mon in Sep, 4th Thu in Nov, Dec 24–25
- 🍴 Drinks/pastries handcart in atrium ($); good restaurant next door ($$); several restaurants in nearby Colony Square office complex
- Ⓜ Arts Center (N5)
- 🚌 10, 23, 35, 36, 98, 148
- ♿ Excellent
- 💵 Moderate (special exhibits often have an additional charge); free Thu after 1PM
- ➡ Atlanta Botanical Garden (➤ 44), Center for Puppetry Arts (➤ 45)
- ❓ Special exhibit tours. Gift shop

43

21

ATLANTA BOTANICAL GARDEN

HIGHLIGHTS

- Rooster topiary creation
- Poison-arrow frogs display
- Vanilla orchid vine on cacao tree
- Storza Woods
- Waterfall in conservatory
- Double coconut seed (largest in plant kingdom)
- "Living stones" desert plants
- Japanese Garden
- Lily-pond stone carvings
- Carnivorous plant bog

INFORMATION

The Atlanta Botanical Garden is an oasis in this busy city. You can admire the flowers—different at every season—hike in the woods, or wander through the many and varied natural environments found in the conservatory.

The Atlanta Botanical Garden is composed of three separate areas: landscaped gardens, virgin forest, and a conservatory.

The gardens The landscaped outdoor gardens, spread over 15 acres, exhibit more than 3,000 different plants, including a rose garden, traditional Japanese garden with bridge and goldfish pond, English herb garden, southern vegetable garden, dwarf and rare conifer garden, fragrance garden for the blind, and a rock garden.

Storza Woods This 15-acre preserved hardwood forest has paved trails where you can view plants native to Georgia in their natural setting. Its "Upper Woodland" section, especially beautiful from April to June when native Georgian flowering shrubs and trees are in full bloom, features a backyard wildlife habitat and a fern glade with recycling stream.

Dorothy Chapman Fuqua Conservatory Flora from various desert and tropical habitats, as well

as endangered plant species, are grown here in a fascinating computer-controlled environment. Huge leaves provide a canopy over walkways, and the whole effect is further enhanced by waterfalls and chirping birds.

CENTER FOR PUPPETRY ARTS

Puppetry is not just for children. After a visit here you will discover that it is a sophisticated and interesting form of entertainment that requires craftsmanship, mechanical ability, and acting skill. Above all, it will make you laugh.

The Center for Puppetry Arts is one of only two facilities in the United States specializing in this Old World entertainment medium and art form. Since opening in 1978, it has expanded public awareness about puppetry through a variety of educational and entertainment programs.

Education The history and use of puppets is best explained at the center's International Puppet Museum, a fascinating collection of over 200 hand, string, rod, and shadow puppets that span several centuries and cultures. It includes miniature pre-Columbian clay puppets, ritualistic African figures, Punch and Judy from France, and the Muppets Kermit the Frog and Miss Piggy, America's best-loved puppets. PuppetWorks, a hands-on exhibit, allows visitors to operate similar puppets, while the Animatronics display introduces visitors to new technologies via radio-controlled puppets.

Entertainment With four theaters—up-close and intimate to a 300-seater—puppetry is presented regularly by black-clothed professional puppeteers who might use rod puppets, full body puppets, hand puppets, or the classic marionette. Classic tales such as *Pinocchio* and *Cinderella* hold your children spellbound, while Shakespearian dramas, the New Directions series, and Xperimental Puppetry Theater present adult themes. A behind-the-scenes look at the puppeteers is included in some programs.

HIGHLIGHTS

- Live puppet theater
- Kermit the Frog Muppet
- Pigs in Space Muppets
- Jim Henson (Muppet creator) tribute exhibit
- Trash Phoenix
- PuppetWorks
- Puppet Storeroom
- German scarf puppet
- Punch and Judy
- Animatronics

INFORMATION

- F3
- 1404 Spring Street at 16th Street
- Recorded information: 404/873–3391
- Museum: Mon–Sat 9–4. Performances: times vary. Closed Jan 1, Easter Mon, last Mon in May, Jul 4, 1st Mon in Sep, 4th Thu in Nov, Dec 24–25
- Arts Center (N5)
- Good
- Museum: inexpensive. Performances: moderate
- High Museum of Art (➤ 43)
- Gift shop, regular workshops

23

ATLANTA HISTORY CENTER

HIGHLIGHTS

- Swan House
- Civil War collection
- Tullie Smith Farm
- Battle of Atlanta exhibit
- Folk life exhibit
- *Gone with the Wind* gallery
- Costume collection
- Swan Woods Trail
- Asian-American Gardens
- Farm animals

INFORMATION

- ✚ Off map at F1
- ✉ 130 West Paces Ferry Road
- ☎ 404/814–4000 (recorded information on this line after closing hours)
- ◷ Mon–Sat 10–5:30; Sun noon–5. Closed Jan 1, 4th Thu in Nov, Dec 24–25
- 🍴 Good café ($) in museum; restaurant ($) near Swan House
- 🚇 Lenox (N7), then bus 23; or Lindbergh (N6), then bus 40; or West Lake (W4), then bus 58
- ♿ Few
- 💲 Expensive
- ↔ Georgia Governor's Mansion (➤ 47), Buckhead (➤ 58)
- ❓ Swan House tours. Regular series of lectures, workshops, programs, and festivals, and annual events such as Civil War Encampment weekend

The Tullie Smith farmhouse

The best way to enjoy this center—and the only way to understand fully what you have seen—is to take it in small chunks. There is just too much visual stimulation to cram it all into one day. Among its many sights, don't miss the Swan House.

The Atlanta History Center, a 32-acre complex in the prestigious Buckhead neighborhood, is dedicated to preserving, protecting, and displaying the history of Atlanta.

History retold The Museum of Atlanta History, opened in 1993, is an awesome collection of documents, clothes, and artifacts that honors Atlanta's heritage since 1835. The permanent exhibition tells Atlanta's complete history, with separate galleries devoted to specific events. The Civil War gallery has nearly 26,000 items, including 800 weapons. Next door in McElreath Hall are the center's archives and library, and an exhibition devoted to the Battle of Atlanta.

Contrasting homes Also on the 32-acre site is Swan House, a classical-style mansion designed by noted architect Philip Shutze in 1926 and owned by a rich cotton broker. Inside, the house is a veritable museum of decorative arts. The

Tullie Smith Farm, a two-story farmhouse (1845) with outbuildings brought here from another Atlanta location, features barnyard animals and farm-life demonstrations. Seven interconnecting gardens and hiking trails make up the rest of the grounds.

GEORGIA GOVERNOR'S MANSION

The Georgia Governor's Mansion, with its white Doric column portico, is reminiscent of the plantation houses found in the rural South. You can easily imagine Rhett Butler coming here to sweep Scarlett off her feet.

Exterior The Georgia Governor's Mansion, completed in 1968 and set in sprawling grounds with many formal flower and shrubbery gardens, is the official residence of the Governor of Georgia. The 24,000-square foot, two-story Greek Revival-styled house—located on top of a hill in the middle of an 18-acre plot—is similar to the first governor's mansion built in Milledgeville (central Georgia) in 1838, and more closely resembles a Mississippi plantation house than a Georgian *ante bellum* mansion. The red-brick rectangular shape is completely wrapped by a white Doric column portico, with its front entrance based on a 1930s design by Asher Benjamin.

Current furnishings Inside the mansion, the beautiful 19th-century furnishings, paintings, and porcelain (including one of the finest collections of Federal Period furniture in the United States) reflect the formality and grandeur of the office. A large bronze state seal inlaid in the white marble floor dominates the entrance to the mansion. Since the furnishings are valuable, tour visitors are not allowed in the actual rooms, but must stand at roped entrances to them while a guide explains the historical significance of each item. The tour includes all the rooms of the first floor and the Circular Hall, the latter decorated with an early 19th-century Italian chandelier, a full-length portrait of George Washington, and a rare French vase with a Benjamin Franklin portrait medallion.

HIGHLIGHTS

- Benjamin Franklin vase
- George Washington portrait
- Georgia-made huntboard (family dining room)
- Italian chandelier
- Alcove bed (guest bedroom)
- Scroll-arm sofas (family living room)
- Silver service (state dining room)
- Library
- Front entrance (exterior)
- Chinese glass paintings (family living room)

INFORMATION

- ✚ Off map at F1
- ✉ 391 West Paces Ferry Road
- ☎ 404/261–1776.
  Recorded information:
  404/261–1858
- 🕐 Guided tours: Tue–Thu 10–11:30
- 🍴 Dozens of restaurants in nearby Buckhead business area
- 🚌 Lenox (N7), then bus 23; or Lindbergh (N6), then bus 40; or West Lake (W4), then bus 58
- ♿ Very good
- ✋ Free
- ↔ Atlanta History Center (► 46), Buckhead (► 58)
- ❓ Candlelight tours during Christmas season. Reservations required for groups over 20

25

MICHAEL C. CARLOS MUSEUM

HIGHLIGHTS

- Egyptian mummies
- Floor stencils
- Pre-Columbian collection
- Roman coins
- Re-created Jericho excavation site
- Native American exhibit
- Cuneiform tablets
- Plaster re-creations of ancient architectural details
- "Goddess of the West" coffin painting

INFORMATION

- Off map at K2
- 571 Kilgo Street at Emory University
- Recorded information/voice mail: 404/727–4282
- Mon–Thu, Sat 10–5; Fri 10–9; Sun noon–5. Closed Jan 1, Easter Mon, last Mon in May, Jul 4, 1st Mon in Sep, 4th Thu in Nov, Dec 24–25
- Good restaurant on upper level ($$)
- Edgewood–Candler Park (E4), then bus 6; or Arts Center (N5), then bus 36
- Good
- Free; suggested donation
- Fernbank Museum of Natural History (➤ 36), Fernbank Science Center (➤ 37)
- Group tours. Gift shop, annual Before Christ Fest, regular lectures, films, workshops, and special traveling exhibitions

While you're looking up at the exhibits, look down at the floor, too, where stenciled diagrams help you understand the item's place in history. It may be the floor plan of an ancient mortuary temple or the meandering course of the Nile River.

Post-modern exhibition space The Michael C. Carlos Museum is a combination art, ancient history, and archaeological museum with over 15,000 pieces in its permanent collection. It is housed in a 1916 Beaux Arts building on the Emory University campus (Atlanta's most prestigious private college). Its contemporary interior, designed by the renowned architect Michael Graves, is a showcase in itself.

Ancient history The strength of this collection are early antiquities dating to 300 B.C. excavated from Middle Eastern countries, including artifacts from the ancient site of Babylon, Bronze and Iron Age pottery, oil lamps from Palestine, and a good collection of Egyptian mummies complete with their gold coffins and the treasures found inside them. Throughout the museum, periods of history and the process of archaeology are re-created with artifacts and photographic displays, such as the replica of the excavation site at Jericho, filled with the remains of 25 human skeletons; and the excavation of pharaoh burial sites in Egypt. There is also an excellent art and antique collection from early A.D. civilizations such as Rome, Central and South America, Mesopotamia, and Native American tribes. Its pre-Columbian collection comprises 1,300 objects, including gold jewelry, pottery, and statues. It also has a sizable collection of drawings, prints, and illustrated manuscripts from the Middle Ages to the present day, as well as a few French Impressionist paintings.

ATLANTA
best

MODERN ARCHITECTURE

A great architect

A great portion of Atlanta's modern Downtown skyline is the work of home-grown architect John Portman, who was educated at the Georgia Institute of Technology. His most famous structures are the Westin Peachtree Plaza Hotel, Atlanta Merchandise Mart, Gift Mart and Apparel Mart, Peachtree Center, Inforum, Hyatt Regency Atlanta Hotel, and One Peachtree Center.

The dramatic Downtown skyline

See Top 25 Sights for
HIGH MUSEUM OF ART (1983) ➤ 43

ATLANTA MARRIOTT MARQUIS (1985)

The unusually designed 48-story-high atrium, with walls that taper inwards the higher you go and a curvy balcony railing on each level, resembles the rib cage of a prehistoric animal. A gigantic fabric sculpture by French artist Daniel Graffin hangs within it.
🚹 F6　✉ 265 Peachtree Center Avenue　☎ 404/521–0000
🕐 24-hour hotel　🍴 Five restaurants, four bars　🚇 Peachtree Center (N1)

BUCKHEAD PLAZA BUILDING (1987)

At the heart of the Buckhead business district, this narrow, 19-story, neo-Gothic office tower has a gabled top and flying buttresses that extend downward from the third level. Alternating bands of green reflective glass and polished pink Canadian granite adorn its exterior walls.
🚹 Off map at F1　✉ 3116 Peachtree Road　🕐 Offices: business hours only. Stores: 9–9　🍴 Good restaurants at lower level　🚇 23

FULTON COUNTY ADMINISTRATION COMPLEX (1989)

This airy and futuristic building is a Postmodern brick and glass structure composed of several units of differing heights connected to a central glass atrium. Its pseudo-ancient Grecian lobby, with palm trees, a sunken fountain, and a columned archway, offers a contrast to its otherwise modern surroundings.
🚹 F7　✉ 150 Pryor Street　🕐 Business hours only　🍴 Several restaurants and fast-food outlets in nearby Underground Atlanta　🚇 Five Points (O)

GEORGIA-PACIFIC BUILDING (1982)

This rust-red 52-story building, with a stair-stepping pyramid design at the upper levels, occupies hallowed ground on the site of Loew's Grand Theater (burned in 1978), where *Gone with the Wind* was premièred in 1939.
🚹 F6　✉ 133 Peachtree Street　🕐 Business hours only　🍴 Good restaurant ($$$)　🚇 Peachtree Center (N1)

NATIONSBANK PLAZA TOWER (1992)

This 53-story building, visible from many city locations, is the tallest in the South at 1,023 feet. Its conical, multistory, open birdcage-like roof, topped by a large bronze spire, is its most prominent feature.
🖽 F5   ✉ 600 West Peachtree Street   🕐 Business hours only
🍽 Several restaurants in the area   🚇 North Avenue (N3)

ONE ATLANTIC CENTER (1987)

This 50-story, 825-foot-tall, Gothic-inspired office tower was Atlanta's tallest building from 1987 to 1992. Its copper pyramid roof is a city landmark.
🖽 F3   ✉ 1201 West Peachtree Street   🕐 Business hours only
🍽 Several restaurants in nearby Colony Square   🚇 Arts Center (N5)

ONE NINETY ONE PEACHTREE TOWER (1990)

Highly noticeable with its twin-towered neo-classical top, this 52-story office tower is a modern interpretation of the buildings found in America at the turn of the century, and offers a unique contrast to downtown Atlanta's more modern-looking towers. A monumental arched entryway leads into an elaborate, six-story, skylit atrium lobby.
🖽 F6   ✉ 191 Peachtree Street   🕐 Business hours only
🍽 Several restaurants half a block north   🚇 Peachtree Center (N1)

ONE PEACHTREE CENTER TOWER (1992)

This skyscraper features several slender, interconnecting towers of differing heights that form a jumbled, building-block pyramid top 60 stories high. Inside, a two-story lobby entered from four sides bridges a circular reflecting pool.
🖽 F6   ✉ 303 Peachtree Street   🕐 Business hours only
🍽 Excellent restaurant and café   🚇 Peachtree Center (N1)

RIO SHOPPING MALL (1989)

This unusual-looking, two-story, U-shaped structure, with garishly painted corrugated-steel walls, features the most bizarre plaza in the city. Some 350 large, squatting, bronze frogs ride on the surface of a reflecting pool on the front lawn that is lit by submerged fiberoptic strips and surrounds a white tubular sphere.
🖽 G5   ✉ 535 Piedmont Avenue   🕐 9–9 for stores, later for restaurants   🍽 Three restaurants in Mall   🚇 North Avenue (N3)

WESTIN PEACHTREE PLAZA HOTEL (1976)

This 73-story cylindrical tower, sheathed in dark reflective glass, and with its trademark external elevator and post-modern five-story atrium lobby, is the second-tallest hotel in the world and the focal point of the Atlanta skyline. The Sun Dial Restaurant and Lounge (➤ 69) offers great views over Atlanta.
🖽 F6   ✉ 210 Peachtree Street   ☎ 404/659–1400   🕐 24-hour hotel   🍽 Three restaurants, three bars   🚇 Peachtree Center (N1)

Pencil Building

The narrow One Atlantic Center, designed by famed architects John Burgee and Philip Johnson, and with a pointed copper-covered roof and narrow steeple, is known as the "Pencil Building" by many residents. Others refer to it as the "IBM Building" due to its primary occupant. Although several new buildings have sprung up around it in recent years, it is still the most prominent building in the Midtown area of Atlanta.

One Peachtree Center Tower

51

OLDEST BUILDINGS

A 20th-century city

When the Battle of Atlanta ended very few buildings remained standing downtown as most of them had been torched deliberately by Yankee troops. Because of this, Atlanta's architectural history belongs to the 20th century. Churches aside, the oldest buildings date from 1890 to 1930, a period of economic prosperity that saw the construction of the city's first skyscrapers.

The Flatiron Building

52

> **See Top 25 Sights for**
> **HURT COTTAGE (1882)** ➤ 34
> **STATE CAPITOL OF GEORGIA (1889)** ➤ 27
> **TULLIE SMITH FARM (1845)** ➤ 46

BULLOCH HALL (c. 1840)
This large Greek Revival *ante bellum* mansion features a pedimented portico supported by four massive Doric columns.
➕ Off map at F1 ✉ 180 Bulloch Avenue in Roswell ☎ 770/992–1731 🕐 Mon–Fri 10–2 🍴 Several restaurants and fast-food outlets along Roswell Road 🚇 Lenox (N7), then bus 85 💵 Inexpensive ❓ Guided tours

CANDLER BUILDING (1906)
Built for Coca-Cola founder Asa G. Candler, this 17-story building has an elaborately decorated exterior, featuring carved medallions of famous men, and a marble staircase in its lobby.
➕ F6 ✉ 127 Peachtree Street 🕐 Business hours only 🍴 Several restaurants nearby 🚇 Peachtree Center (N1)

CAPITAL CITY CLUB (1911)
The five-story, Italian Renaissance-style house, with projecting twin-columned porches, is home to the city's oldest private club.
➕ F6 ✉ 7 Harris Street 🕐 Members only 🍴 Several restaurants and fast-food outlets in nearby Peachtree Center Mall 🚇 Peachtree Center (N1)

DEKALB COUNTY HISTORIC COMPLEX (1822–1840)
This complex features two *ante bellum*-style houses and the John Biffle Cabin (1822), a restored log and plank structure built by a Revolutionary War veteran.
➕ Off map at K6 ✉ 720 West Trinity Place in Decatur ☎ 404/373–1088 🕐 Mon–Fri 9–4:30 🍴 Several restaurants and fast-food outlets in downtown Decatur 🚇 Decatur (E6) 💵 Free

FLATIRON BUILDING (1897)
This 11-story triangular-shaped building, designed by Bradford Gilbert, was Atlanta's first skyscraper.
➕ F6 ✉ 84 Peachtree Street 🕐 Business hours only 🍴 Café 🚇 Five Points (0), Peachtree Center (N1)

GEORGIA RAILROAD FREIGHT DEPOT (1869)
This building, replacing the one torched by Union troops in the 1864 Battle of Atlanta, is now used as a meeting hall and for special events.
➕ F7 ✉ Depot Plaza (opposite The World of Coca-Cola) 🕐 During special events only 🍴 Several restaurants and fast-food outlets in nearby Underground Atlanta 🚇 Five Points (0)

HAMMONDS HOUSE (1857) ➤ 60

HEALEY BUILDING (1913)

One of Atlanta's most elegant early skyscrapers, built in the neo-Gothic style with Tudor decorations and a rotunda lobby lit by natural light.

➕ F6 ✉ 57 Forsyth Street 🕐 Business hours only 🚇 Five Points (0)

NATIONSBANK BUILDING (1901)

One of the first steel-framed structures built in America, the NationsBank features a sumptuous lobby and banking area with high ceilings, chandeliers, marble floors, and bronze desks.

➕ F6 ✉ 35 Broad Street 🕐 Business hours only 🍴 Café 🚇 Five Points (0)

RHODES MEMORIAL HALL (1904)

Resembling a Rhine River castle with a four-story square tower and turreted roof, this house was built for a wealthy furniture chain-store owner. Its carved mahogany staircase is lined with nine stained-glass window panels depicting Civil War scenes.

➕ F2 ✉ 1516 Peachtree Street ☎ 404/881–9980 🕐 Mon–Fri 11–4 🍴 Several restaurants along Peachtree Street 🚇 Arts Center (N5) 💷 Cheap

SHRINE OF THE IMMACULATE CONCEPTION (1873)

This Gothic-style church, complete with rose window and unequal towers, was built to replace an earlier shrine. The original church was spared by Sherman's troops after an impassioned plea by its pastor, Thomas O'Reilly, whose tomb is in the basement.

➕ F7 ✉ 48 Martin Luther King, Jr. Drive 🕐 Daily 9–6; later when there are special events 🍴 Several restaurants and fast-food outlets in nearby Underground Atlanta 🚇 Five Points (0)

STONE MOUNTAIN PARK PLANTATION (1790–1845)

Within Stone Mountain Park (➤ 38) are 19 plantation buildings brought from other Georgia locations, including an 18th-century house, an 1845 *ante bellum* mansion, slave quarters, and a barn (1800).

➕ Off map at K4 ✉ East on US 78 (look for exit signs for Stone Mountain Park) ☎ 770/498–5600 🕐 Sep–May daily 10–5:30. Jun–Aug daily 10–9 🍴 Several restaurants ($$) and food concessions ($) throughout the park 🚇 Avondale (E7), then bus 120 💷 Expensive (includes park entrance fee plus plantation entrance fee)

WIMBISH HOUSE (1898)

A French château look-alike with a steep mansard roof and turreted corner rooms. This is one of the few houses left on Peachtree Street; now a dance club.

➕ G3 ✉ 1150 Peachtree Street 🕐 Not open to public during the day 🍴 Several restaurants in nearby Colony Square 🚇 Midtown (N4), Arts Center (N5)

Progress?

Atlanta has suffered from two potentially disastrous forces. The first was a Union general with a mission to destroy Atlanta. Fortunately, he had tunnel vision and missed many buildings in the outlying areas. The other force is modern progress, whose developers value prime tracts of land over historical buildings. Due to the efforts of various preservation societies, however, many historical buildings have been moved to protected sites.

A stained-glass window in Rhodes Memorial Hall

SMALL & UNIQUE MUSEUMS

Southeastern Railway Museum

Although it lies off the beaten track, the Southeastern Railway Museum is a must-see for train fanatics, with a collection of 40 steam and diesel locomotives, passenger and freight cars, and over 7,000 items of train memorabilia displayed in a former postal van. Its pride and joy is a scaled-down steam train which takes children for a ten-minute ride through a tunnel and over a bridge (🔶 Off map at G1 ✉ 3966 Buford Highway (U.S. 23) in Duluth ☎ 770/476–2013 🕐 Sat 9–5 🎫 Inexpensive ❓ Accessible only by car).

APEX (AFRICAN-AMERICAN PANORAMIC EXPERIENCE) ➤ 60

FEDERAL RESERVE MONETARY MUSEUM
This museum explains the history of money through Native American trading beads, gem-stones, a 27-pound gold bar and $100,000 bills. You get a complimentary packet of shredded bills to take home.
🔶 F6 ✉ 104 Marietta Street ☎ 404/521–8764 🕐 Mon–Fri 9–4 🍴 Cafés along Marietta Street; restaurants and fast food in Underground Atlanta, five blocks away 🚇 Five Points (0) 🎫 Free

GEORGIA STATE MUSEUM OF SCIENCE AND INDUSTRY
This odd collection includes a mounted two-headed cow, squirrels playing poker and other stuffed animals, plus displays of Georgia minerals, agricultural items, Native American artifacts, and military rifles.
🔶 F7 ✉ 206 Washington Street in the State Capitol of Georgia (➤ 27) ☎ 404/656–2000 🕐 Mon–Fri 8:30–5; Sat 10–4; Sun noon–4. Closed all federal and state holidays 🍴 Cafeteria in building opposite 🚇 Georgia State (E1) 🎫 Free

HIGH MUSEUM OF ART FOLK ART AND PHOTOGRAPHY GALLERIES
This annex of the larger High Museum of Art (➤ 43) exhibits American folk art and photography from its permanent collection and traveling shows.
🔶 F6 ✉ 30 John Wesley Dobbs Avenue in Georgia-Pacific Building (➤ 50) ☎ 404/577–6940 🕐 Mon–Sat 10–5 🍴 Good restaurants north on Peachtree Street 🚇 Peachtree Center (N1) 🎫 Free

One of the many engines preserved in the Southeastern Railway Museum

MERCER MUSIC COLLECTION
Johnny Mercer, the songwriter who penned "Old Black Magic" and "Moon River," is honored here. Posters, record-album covers, photographs, and his Grammy and Oscar awards are on display.
🔶 F7 ✉ 103 Decatur Street in Pullen Library South, 8th floor ☎ 404/651–2477 🕐 Mon–Fri 8:30–5 🚇 Georgia State (E1) 🎫 Free

TELEPHONE MUSEUM
The history of Alexander Graham Bell's invention, from its earliest inception to current telestar and fiberoptic technology, is explained through various exhibits and a 15-minute movie.
🔶 F4 ✉ 675 West Peachtree Street, second floor (plaza level) in BellSouth Center ☎ 404/223–3661 🕐 Mon–Fri 11–1 🍴 Cafeteria 🚇 North Avenue (N3; entrance into BellSouth building) 🎫 Free

BATTLE OF ATLANTA SITES

**See Top 25 Sights for
OAKLAND CEMETERY ➤ 33**

DEGRESS AVENUE BATTERY
On July 22, 1864, fierce fighting occurred when a Confederate brigade overran a Union artillery battery. The troops were repulsed later that day after General Sherman spotted the attack from Copenhill (➤ 35). Historical markers guide you through the battle.
⊞ J/K6 ⊠ Degress Avenue at DeKalb Avenue ⏱ 24 hours (avoid at night) 🍴 Several restaurants in nearby Little Five Points business district (➤ 18) 🚇 Inman Park–Reynoldstown (E3)

ETERNAL FLAME OF THE CONFEDERACY
Opposite Underground Atlanta (➤ 29), look for an old-fashioned gas street light, restored and returned to the site where a shell bounced off its post in 1864, exploding and fatally wounding a black barber.
⊞ F7 ⊠ Upper Alabama Street at Peachtree Street ⏱ 24 hours (avoid after midnight) 🍴 Several restaurants and fast-food outlets in Underground Atlanta 🚇 Five Points (O)

FORT WALKER
The remains of a Confederate artillery breastwork (with cannon) and defensive earthworks dug by slaves can be seen southeast of Cyclorama (➤ 25). The fort is named after General W. Walker, killed near here.
⊞ H9 ⊠ Boulevard at Delmar Avenue in Grant Park ⏱ 24 hours (avoid at night) 🚌 31, 32 💵 Free

KENNESAW MOUNTAIN NATIONAL BATTLEFIELD PARK ➤ 20

MCPHERSON MONUMENT
An upturned cannon monument marks the spot where Union General James B. McPherson, one of Sherman's top commanders, was killed on July 22, 1864.
⊞ K8 ⊠ McPherson Avenue at Monument Avenue ⏱ 24 hours (avoid at night) 🚌 7

TANYARD CREEK PARK/COLLIER ROAD/PEACHTREE CREEK
It was in this area on July 20, 1864, that Confederate troops, detecting a gap in the Union line, staged a massive assault. After two hours of heavy fighting, they were driven back. Historical markers tell the story.
⊞ E1 ⊠ Collier Road halfway between Peachtree Road and Northside Drive ⏱ 24 hours (avoid at night) 🍴 Several restaurants along Peachtree Road 🚌 23

Killed in battle
During the night of July 21, 1864, weary Confederate troops withdrew from Peachtree Creek with orders to march toward Decatur, where they could launch a surprise rear attack on the Union army. Instead, they encountered the fast-advancing Union flank at dawn. By the end of the day on July 22, over 6,000 Confederate and 4,000 Union soldiers lay dead.

This marker in Kennesaw Mountain National Battlefield Park outlines a key stage in the Battle of Atlanta, 1864

ATTRACTIONS FOR CHILDREN

Something for everyone

Whatever your budget, there is something in Atlanta that will entertain or educate your children. If you choose the very expensive theme parks, be prepared to have fun yourself as some of the rides and attractions are designed specifically for adults. To get your money's worth and to sample all the rides, plan on staying the entire day.

AMERICAN ADVENTURES & WHITE WATER ATLANTA

These two adjoining theme parks are a kid's dream come true. The former has an elaborate tree house costing over $1 million, 15 indoor and outdoor rides, miniature golf, a race-car track, and Imagination Station to keep your children busy for hours. The latter has 40 water attractions, including the largest kids' water playground in the country.

➕ Off map at D1 ✉ 250 North Cobb Parkway in Marietta ☎ 770/424–9283 🕐 Jun–Sep Mon–Thu 11–7; Fri–Sun 10–9. Rest of year hours vary, so call in advance 💵 Very expensive ♿ Accessible only by car

CHATTAHOOCHEE NATURE CENTER

Children of all ages will enjoy seeing the animals, birds, and other creatures kept here in their natural habitats. Nature trails and boardwalks wind through 100 acres of woodlands and wetlands bordering the Chattahoochee River.

➕ Off map at F1 ✉ 9135 Willeo Road ☎ 770/992–2055 🕐 Daily 9–5 🚇 Lenox (N7), then bus 85 💵 Cheap

SIX FLAGS OVER GEORGIA

This is Atlanta's oldest theme park, and has more than 100 rides, many of them heart-stopping roller coasters (one goes in an upside-down loop). Leave the water rides until last to save being damp all day. The park also features musical revues, high-diving demonstrations, and concerts by national artists.

➕ Off map at A7 ✉ I-20W at 7561 Six Flags Road in Austell ☎ 770/739–3400 🕐 Jun–mid-Sep daily 10–10. Mar–May, mid-Sep–Oct Sat–Sun 10–10. Closed Nov–Feb 🍴 Several cafés, snacks areas 🚇 Hightower (W5), then Six Flags shuttle bus 201 💵 Very expensive

SOUTHEASTERN RAILWAY MUSEUM ➤ 54

YELLOW RIVER GAME RANCH

This 24-acre ranch is home to deer, rabbits, and an assortment of farm animals, all waiting to be fed and petted. Trails lead to a series of animal viewing areas, where you may spot buffalo, cougar, fox, skunk, porcupine, bobcat, and other wild creatures.

➕ Off map at K4 ✉ 4525 Highway 78 in Lilburn ☎ 770/972–6643 🕐 Oct–May daily 9:30–6. Jun–Sep daily 9:30–9 💵 Moderate ♿ Accessible only by car

Six Flags Over Georgia

FREE ATTRACTIONS

See Top 25 Sights for
FERNBANK SCIENCE CENTER ➤ 37
GEORGIA GOVERNOR'S MANSION ➤ 47
INMAN PARK ➤ 34
MARTIN LUTHER KING, JR. TOMB IN
THE COURTYARD OF THE CENTER FOR
NON-VIOLENT SOCIAL CHANGE ➤ 32
MICHAEL C. CARLOS MUSEUM ➤ 48
OAKLAND CEMETERY ➤ 33
STATE CAPITOL OF GEORGIA ➤ 27
UNDERGROUND ATLANTA ➤ 29

SMALL MUSEUMS FOR FREE ➤ 54
Federal Reserve Monetary Museum
Georgia State Museum of Science and Industry
High Museum of Art Folk Art and Photography
Galleries
Mercer Music Collection
Telephone Museum

OTHER CATEGORIES WITH FREE ATTRACTIONS
Modern Architecture ➤ 50–51
Oldest Buildings ➤ 52–53
Battle of Atlanta Sites ➤ 55
Intown Neighborhoods ➤ 58
Parks & Forests ➤ 59

ATLANTA CELEBRITY WALK
The names of famous Georgians such as Ray
Charles and Jimmy Carter are etched into a marble
walkway, Atlanta's version of the Hollywood Walk
of Fame.
➕ F6 ✉ 235 International Boulevard (in front of Atlanta Chamber of
Commerce building) 🕐 24 hours (avoid at night) 🍴 Restaurants in
CNN Center opposite 🚇 Omni/Dome/GWCC (W1)

ATLANTA JOURNAL & CONSTITUTION GALLERY
An old type machine, front page news documenting
historic events, and photographs of famous
individuals who have worked for the city's daily
newspaper.
➕ F6 ✉ 72 Marietta Street ☎ 404/526–5151 🕐 Mon–Fri 8–5
🚇 Five Points (0)

SWEET AUBURN CURB MARKET
Markets provide a good look at local traditions.
This one specializes in southern "soul" foods such
as collards, turnip greens, chitterlings, boiled
peanuts, and every edible part of a pig but the
oink. Come to observe and—if you dare—sample
some food.
➕ J6 ✉ 209 Edgewood Avenue ☎ 404/659–1665
🕐 Mon–Sat 8–5:45 🍴 Café and deli food service; individual vendors
🚌 17, 99

The City of Trees
Atlanta is called the City of Trees
as its beautiful neighborhoods are
lined with massive oak and
dogwood trees that shelter the
streets and homes. The word
Peachtree is used in more than
56 street designations throughout
metropolitan Atlanta and in
several business names. It
was derived through a
misinterpretation of the Creek
Indian word for "pitch," the sap
from pine trees that you are more
apt to find here than the fruit
tree, which grows better
elsewhere in the South.

INTOWN NEIGHBORHOODS

See Top 25 Sights for INMAN PARK ➤ 34

The best addresses

To live in Buckhead means instant prestige. As the city's most sought-after address it also has some of the most loosely defined boundaries, the result being the spawning of sub-Buckhead neighborhoods such as SoBuck (south Buckhead), known for its abundance of art and antiques galleries, and younger, trendier residents. The main route through Buckhead is Peachtree Road, north of I-85.

ANSLEY PARK

This is one of Atlanta's most respected neighborhoods, with large homes set back on hilly, landscaped lots. Developed in 1904–1913, it quickly became a suburb for upper-class families.
🔢 G2/3   ✉ Just east of the High Museum of Art (➤ 43), bounded by 15th Street, Peachtree Street, Beverly Road, Piedmont Avenue   🍴 Several restaurants along Peachtree Street   🚇 Arts Center (N5)

BUCKHEAD

A large percentage of Atlanta's wealthy citizens live here: over 105 million-dollar homes are found along the streets near the Governor's Mansion. Its main business district has the city's most interesting chic shops, restaurants and nightclubs.
🔢 Off map at F1   ✉ Peachtree Road, East Paces and West Paces Ferry Roads, Roswell Road intersection (business district)   🕐 9–9 for stores, later for clubs, theaters, and restaurants   🍴 Numerous restaurants and cafés in Buckhead business district   🚌 23, 38, 40, 58

DRUID HILLS

Immaculate flower beds, shrubbery, and dogwood trees make this one of Atlanta's prettiest neighborhoods in the spring. It was developed in the early 1900s by Joel Hurt (of Inman Park fame) and renowned landscape architect Frederick Law Olmsted.
🔢 K4 and off map at K4   ✉ Bounded by Briarcliff Road, Fairview Road, The By Way, Clifton Road   🚌 2, 6

MIDTOWN

The Midtown business district skyline is comparable to the one downtown, while the renovated mansions in its residential section make it a city showcase.
🔢 F/G4   ✉ Bounded by Ponce de Leon Avenue, Monroe Drive, Peachtree Street, 10th Street   🍴 Several restaurants along boundary streets   🚇 North Avenue (N3), Midtown (N4)

VIRGINIA-HIGHLAND

After a decade of young professionals buying and renovating homes in the area, Virginia-Highland is now the hot neighborhood to live in. The galleries, stores, bars, restaurants, and music clubs in its business district compete with Buckhead's.
🔢 J3   ✉ Virginia Avenue at North Highland Avenue (business district)   🕐 9–9 for stores, later for clubs, theaters, and restaurants   🍴 Several restaurants   🚌 16, 45

A Druid Hills mansion

PARKS & FORESTS

CENTENNIAL OLYMPIC PARK
The 21-acre park is a beautiful landscaped area created from a decrepit warehouse district. Check out the five-ring Olympic fountain and the Olympic theme sculpture. The surface is paved with bricks engraved with the names of Olympic contributors.
🔲 F6 ✉ Between Atlanta Gift Mart and Inforum buildings via International Boulevard to CNN Center ⏰ 24 hours (avoid at night) 🍴 Restaurants in Peachtree Center 🚇 Peachtree Center (N1)

CHASTAIN MEMORIAL PARK
This park is best known for its outdoor amphitheater, where nationally renowned musicians—classical, folk, rock, and jazz performers—play in summer concerts. It also has a golf course and other recreational facilities.
🔲 Off map at F1 ✉ 4469 Stella Drive ☎ Concert information: 404/233–7275. Tickets: 404/249–6400 ⏰ Varies depending on concert 🍴 Snack bars 🚌 38 💲 Park: free. Concerts: very expensive

CHATTAHOOCHEE NATURE CENTER
A large portion of the Chattahoochee River that slices through the north and west part of Atlanta, along with the land adjoining it, is protected by the federal government. Its 70 miles of trails range from flat and easy walks along the river to steep, strenuous climbs up river bluffs.
🔲 Off map at F1 ✉ 9135 Willeo Road, Roswell ☎ 770/992–2055 ⏰ Daily 9–5 💲 Free ♿ Accessible only by car

PIEDMONT PARK
Atlanta's largest public park (closed to traffic) is very popular for jogging, bicycling, rollerblading, tennis, and other sports. Free concerts, festivals, and other events are held here throughout the year.
🔲 G/H3 ✉ Piedmont Avenue between 10th and 14th Streets ⏰ 24 hours (avoid at night) 🍴 Several restaurants nearby on 10th Street and Monroe Drive 🚌 31

WOODRUFF PARK
The largest green space in downtown Atlanta. On warm weekdays the park is filled with an interesting mix of office workers, street preachers, politicians, protesters, students, and homeless people.
🔲 F6 ✉ Peachtree Street at Edgewood Avenue ⏰ 24 hours (avoid at night) 🍴 Several restaurants and fast-food eateries at nearby Underground Atlanta 🚇 Five Points (0)

Green spaces
Throughout the city parks of all sizes provide oases of peace and room to play. Piedmont Park sets the standard. Its annual events draw people from afar, and it provides enough open space so that you seldom feel crowded.

Fishing in the Chattahoochee River

AFRICAN-AMERICAN ATTRACTIONS

**See Top 25 Sights for
SWEET AUBURN ► 32**

The Herndon Home

ALONZO F. HERNDON HOME
This 15-room, Georgia Revival-style house (1910) exhibits the decorative furnishings, art collection and other family memorabilia of Atlanta's first black millionaire.

🔳 D6 ⊠ 587 University Place ☎ 404/581–9813 🕐 Tue–Sat 10–4 🍴 Student cafeteria in Atlanta University complex 🚇 Vine City (W2) 💷 Free

APEX (AFRICAN-AMERICAN PANORAMIC EXPERIENCE)
The history and culture of African-Americans in the United States is detailed here through permanent and temporary art and historical exhibits.

🔳 G6 ⊠ 135 Auburn Avenue ☎ 404/521–2739 🕐 Tue–Sat 10–5 🚌 3, 74 💷 Inexpensive

EBENEZER BAPTIST CHURCH
This church was the spiritual center for the 1960s Civil Rights movement and the site of Martin Luther King, Jr.'s funeral. Three generations of Kings preached from its pulpit.

🔳 G6 ⊠ 407 Auburn Avenue ☎ 404/688–7263 🕐 Mon–Fri 9–4:30; Sat 11–2 🚌 3 💷 Free

HAMMONDS HOUSE GALLERIES
The former mansion (1857) of the black anesthetist and arts patron, Otis T. Hammonds, is used as a gallery to display his African-American and Haitian art collection, and as a resource center for African culture.

🔳 C7 ⊠ 503 Peeples Street ☎ 404/752–8730 🕐 Tue–Fri 10–6; Sat–Sun 1–5 🚌 81 💷 Inexpensive

MARTIN LUTHER KING, JR.'S BIRTHPLACE
Martin Luther King, Jr. was born in this modest Queen Anne-style house on January 15, 1929.

🔳 H6 ⊠ 501 Auburn Avenue ☎ 404/331–1590; 404/331–3919 🕐 Daily 10–5 🚌 3 💷 Inexpensive

THE ROYAL PEACOCK
Still a popular music club, the Royal Peacock was frequented in the late 1930s by jazz and blues greats such as Count Basie, Louis Armstrong, and Big Mabel, and in the 1960s by the king and queen of soul—James Brown and Aretha Franklin. Reggae and hip hop are played today.

🔳 G6 ⊠ 186 1/2 Auburn Avenue ☎ 404/880–0745 🕐 Daily 4PM–2AM 🍴 Drinks, snacks 🚌 3, 74 💷 Cover charge

Atlanta's black heritage
Atlanta's history is tied directly to the role of black Americans, especially the 1960s Civil Rights movement leaders whose impassioned speeches were heard every week in Auburn Avenue churches and meeting halls. Today their efforts are being carried forward by black mayors and other politicians who have governed the city for the past two decades.

ATLANTA
where to...

DEEP SOUTH FARE

Prices

Average meal per head, excluding drinks:

$ = up to $15

$$ = up to $35

$$$ = over $35

Southern style— from grits to iced tea

Southern foods are unique to this region. You won't routinely find grits (coarsely ground corn cooked until creamy soft), barbecue (pit roasted chicken, pork or beef served with a tangy sauce), pot likker (liquid left from cooking vegetables), or collard greens (a leafy dark green vegetable) on menus anywhere else in America.

BURTON'S GRILL ($)

Exceptional fried chicken, hoe cakes, iced tea, and southern vegetables attract a regular clientele ranging from blue-collar workers to executives. Get here early or you'll have to wait for a table.

✚ J6 ✉ 1029 Edgewood Avenue opposite station ☎ 404/523–1929 ◉ 6–4 ⍟ Inman Park–Reynoldstown (E3) 🚊 17

THE COLONNADE ($)

Established in 1927, this Atlanta eating institution serves up some of the most authentic southern-style food anywhere. Cornish game hens, country fried steak, frog's legs, and mouthwatering, made-from-scratch desserts keep this place constantly packed.

✚ Off map at H1 ✉ 1879 Cheshire Bridge Road ☎ 404/874–5642 ◉ Mon–Sat 11–2:30, 5–9; Sun 11–9 🚊 27

KUDZU CAFE ($$)

Named after the broad-leafed vine that grows vigorously throughout the South, this restaurant offers updated southern cuisine, and traditional favorites such as fried green tomatoes, grilled meat loaf, and moon pies. Good food, a mountain lodge atmosphere, and a Buckhead address make this a popular dining establishment.

✚ Off map at F1 ✉ 3215 Peachtree Road ☎ 404/262–0661 ◉ Sun–Thu 11–11; Fri–Sat 11AM–midnight 🚊 23

MARY MAC'S TEA ROOM ($)

This restaurant—serving specialties such as fried chicken, black eyed peas, sweet potato pie, cheese grits, and collard greens— is the place to see and to be seen as all classes of people frequent it.

✚ G5 ✉ 224 Ponce de Leon Avenue ☎ 404/876–1800 ◉ Mon–Fri 11–8 ⍟ North Avenue (N3) 🚊 2

PASCHAL'S ($)

Inexpensive southern "soul" food makes this a landmark restaurant. It was one of Martin Luther King, Jr.'s favorite places to dine.

✚ E7 ✉ 830 Martin Luther King, Jr. Drive ☎ 404/577–3150 ◉ 5–midnight ⍟ Vine City (W2) 🚊 3, 53

SILVER GRILL ($)

This small diner serves up home-style southern cooking of the Old South. Excellent fried chicken, mashed potatoes and gravy, grilled pork chops, and vegetables.

✚ H4 ✉ 900 Monroe Drive ☎ 404/876–8145 ◉ Mon–Fri 10:30–9 🚊 27, 45

SILVER SKILLET ($)

Come here for breakfasts of ham, eggs, grits, red-eyed gravy, and homemade biscuits, or lunch specials of fried chicken, home-made corn bread, and other southern foods.

✚ F3 ✉ 200 14th Street ☎ 404/874–1388 ◉ Mon–Fri 6–3; Sat 7–1; Sun 8–2 ⍟ Arts Center (N5) 🚊 98

BURGERS, STEAKS, & BEYOND

BACCHANALIA ($$$)
The contemporary American cuisine with a hint of European flair that emphasizes fresh and healthy ingredients. Goat cheese-potato terrine, venison loin, mini rack of lamb with truffled mashed potatoes, and organically grown coffees are house specialties. It offers a fixed price menu, uncommon in American restaurants.

✚ Off map at H1 ✉ 3125 Piedmont Avenue
☎ 404/365-0410 🕐 Tue–Sat 6PM–10:30PM 🚇 Buckhead (N7) 🚌 5, 38

BLUE RIBBON GRILL ($)
Owned by a local radio personality, who has decorated the walls with photographs of other celebrities, this cozy restaurant features delicious hand-cut steaks, chilli, home-made soups and desserts in a friendly setting.

✚ Off map at K1
✉ 4006 LaVista Road
☎ 770/491-1570
🕐 Mon–Sat 11–2:30, 5:30–11
🚌 125

BONES ($$$)
Considered one of the top ten restaurants in Atlanta, Bones offers near-perfect steaks in any form of cut or size you want, plus a great wine list in a club-like atmosphere. Haughty staff ignore newcomers at times, but you won't find a better steak in town.

✚ Off map at H1
✉ 3130 Piedmont Road
☎ 404/237-2663
🕐 Mon–Fri 11:30–2:30, 6–11; Sat–Sun 6–11 🚇 Buckhead (N7) 🚌 5, 38

BUCKHEAD DINER ($$)
This glittering roadside diner straight out of the 1950s is frequented by a trendy and celebrity crowd. The good-quality American food includes wild mushroom and veal meat loaf, lemon pie, B.L.T., and grilled pork chop with cheese grits.

✚ Off map at H1 ✉ 3073 Piedmont Road
☎ 404/262-3336
🕐 Mon–Sat 11AM–midnight; Sun 11–10 🚇 Buckhead (N7)
🚌 5, 38

MICK'S ($)
This popular and upbeat Atlanta chain has a variety of hamburgers, chicken dishes, salads, and cheesecake desserts to please everyone—all served up in a casual and friendly atmosphere.

✚ F7 ✉ 75 Upper Alabama Street at Underground Atlanta
☎ 404/525-2825 🕐 Daily 11AM–1AM 🚇 Five Points (0)
🚌 3, 13, 17, 20, 42, 90, 97

THE VARSITY ($)
Atlanta's most famous eatery, straight out of the movie *American Graffiti*, has been serving up assembly-line hamburgers, chilli dogs, onion rings, chocolate malts, frosted orange, apple pie, and other typical drive-in fare since the early 1920s. Expanded several times, it still has awning-covered curb service for a few cars. Even if you are a health-food addict, you should eat here at least once.

✚ F5 ✉ 61 North Avenue
☎ 404/881-1706 🕐 Sun–Thu 7AM–12:30AM; Fri–Sat 7AM–2AM 🚇 North Avenue (N3)
🚌 13, 66

Liquid refreshments
Just about anywhere—except for the more upscale restaurants—you'll find that Coca-Cola is king. The drink has been associated with Atlanta for so long that it would be a sacrilege to choose another cola. Remember, too, that if you order tea it will be sweet iced tea unless you specify otherwise.

FRENCH RESTAURANTS

So many choices

Atlanta has one of the most vibrant restaurant scenes in America. With numerous transplants from other regions, plus a burgeoning foreign population, new restaurants sprout up every month featuring new and novel recipes. With so many restaurants to choose from, personal favorites are quickly replaced by something new.

ANIS ($$)

Three Frenchmen who met in Atlanta have created a bistro with excellent food based on traditional Mediterranean and Provençal recipes, specializing in seafood, soups and lamb. Rotating the menu bi-monthly, they offer a hearty *bouillabaisse* seafood stew and duck-lamb cassoulet.

➕ Off map at F1 ✉ 2974 Grand-view Avenue ☎ 404/233–9889 ⏰ Tue–Thu 11:30–2:30, 6–10; Fri–Sat 11:30–2:30, 6–11; Sun 11:30–3, 6–10 🚌 23, 40

BABETTE'S CAFÉ ($$)

This casual bistro-like restaurant, with wood floors and brick walls, serves up European country dishes with an emphasis on French favorites, including a fabulous cassoulet.

➕ J5 ✉ 471 North Highland Avenue ☎ 404/523–9121 ⏰ Tue–Sat 11:30–11; Sun 11:30–4 🚌 16

BRASSERIE LE COZE ($$$)

This is the closest thing in Atlanta to a true Parisian brasserie in terms of both food and décor. Toulouse duck cassoulet, *coq au vin*, *moules à la marinière*, *pot-au-feu*, onion tarts, and fish dishes are delicious and well prepared. Also has delectable desserts and a good wine list.

➕ Off map at K1 ✉ Lenox Square Mall (▶ 70) ☎ 404/266–1440 ⏰ Mon–Thu 11:30–2:30, 5:30–10; Fri–Sat 11:30–11 🚇 Lenox (NE7) 🚌 23, 25, 47, 48, 85, 92, 140

CASSIS ($$)

Named after a small Mediterranean fishing port in France, Cassis specializes in innovative seafood dishes from that area. Grilled, spiced shrimp with aubergine and roasted tomato *coulis*, and mixed grilled seafood with Mediterranean salsa are two house specialties.

➕ Off map at F1 ✉ 3300 Peachtree Road in Hotel Nikko ☎ 404/365–8100 ⏰ Daily 7AM–11PM 🚇 Buckhead (N7) 🚌 5, 23, 38

CIBOULETTE ($$$)

Bistro fare such as Lyonnaise sausage and *choucroute* with lentils, field greens with Roquefort terrine, and liqueur-based desserts are served in an elegant atmosphere with an upper-class, dressy crowd. Open kitchen, mirrored walls, and close tables give it authenticity.

➕ H2 ✉ 1529 Piedmont Avenue ☎ 404/874–7600 ⏰ Mon–Thu 6–10; Fri–Sat 6–11 🚌 31, 36

SOUTH OF FRANCE RESTAURANT ($$)

Owned by three brothers from Nice, this restaurant offers Mediterranean fare such as *bouillabaisse* and other seafood, plus traditional lamb and veal dishes, and the classic onion soup *gratinée*. Its two fireplaces make it cozy on a winter evening.

➕ Off map at H1 ✉ 2345 Cheshire Bridge Road ☎ 404/325–6963 ⏰ Mon–Fri 11:30–2, 6–10:30; Sat 11:30–2, 6–11:30 🚌 6, 27, 30, 33

ITALIAN RESTAURANTS

LA GROTTA RISTORANTE ($$$)

A favorite among Atlanta's best northern Italian restaurants, La Grotta could sit back on its laurels but it doesn't. Try any veal or stuffed pasta dish and you'll leave satisfied. Even simple selections such as angel hair pasta with fresh garlic and basil are superb. Al fresco dining is available on a patio during summer.

✚ Off map at F1
✉ 2637 Peachtree Road
☎ 404/231–1368
🕐 Tue–Sat 6–10:30 🚌 23

LUNA SI ($)

This trendy SoBuck neighborhood café features contemporary Italian cuisine. The menu changes monthly and features unique pasta dishes, fresh seafood, meat and vegetarian selections, all served in an artsy setting.

✚ F2 ✉ 1931 Peachtree Street ☎ 404/355–5993
🕐 Tue–Sun 11–2:30, 5–11
🚇 Arts Center (N5) 🚌 23

PRICCI ($$)

This classy restaurant has a diverse northern Italian menu of recipes from the Tuscan, Ligurian, and Milanese regions, from home-made pastas to seafood, meat and fowl dishes, plus great desserts.

✚ Off map at F1 ✉ 500 Pharr Road ☎ 404/237–2941
🕐 Mon–Thu 11–11; Fri–Sat 11AM–midnight; Sun 5–10
🚌 38, 40

ROCKY'S BRICK OVEN PIZZA & PASTA ($)

Although called a pizzeria, Rocky's is more like a trattoria straight out of Italy, especially with its wood-burning oven imported from Milan, strings of cheese, sausage and garlic hanging from the ceiling, candle-lit tables covered with checked table cloths, classical music, and the variety of Italian dishes on the menu. The chef here uses fresh ingredients and authentic Italian recipes.

✚ F2 ✉ 1770 Peachtree Street ☎ 404/876–1111
🕐 Tue–Thu 11–10:30; Fri 11AM–midnight; Sat–Mon 4PM–midnight 🚇 Arts Center (N5) 🚌 23

SAN GENNARO ($$)

The menu here features classic southern Italian cuisine, including fried calamari and hearty pasta dishes. Sausages and cheeses hanging from the ceiling recall an Italian trattoria. Very popular, so expect a long wait for a table.

✚ Off map at H1 ✉ 2196 Cheshire Bridge Road
☎ 404/636–9447 🕐 Daily 5:30–11 🚌 27

VENI VIDI VICI ($$)

Expect the most superb Italian food here; worth trying in particular are the spit roasted meats and fish dishes, antipasti selections, and huge portions of handmade pasta. The setting is elegant, with an open rotisserie and patio dining outside when the weather is warm.

✚ F3 ✉ 41 14th Street
☎ 404/875–8424
🕐 Mon–Fri 11AM–midnight; Sat–Sun 5PM–midnight 🚇 Arts Center (N5) 🚌 23, 31, 36, 98

Restaurants for romance

La Grotta, with its luxurious interior, checked tablecloths, candles, violinist, and hospitable staff, makes an ideal choice for a romantic evening. San Gennaro is also a good bet for its authentic trattoria look.

SOUTHEAST ASIAN RESTAURANTS

Asian Atlanta

Head for Buford Highway in suburban Chamblee, home of the city's Asian population. Lining this six-lane thoroughfare between Carol Avenue and I-285 (first exit west of I-85) are hundreds of Chinese, Japanese, Thai, Vietnamese, and Korean restaurants, markets, and businesses.

CHA-GIO ($)

Widely acclaimed as one of the best Vietnamese establishments in Atlanta. Spicy chicken (they will make it milder upon request) and vegetarian dishes dominate the menu.
✚ G4 ✉ 132 10th Street
☎ 404/885–9387
🕐 Daily 11–10
🚇 Midtown (N4) 🚌 10

FIRST CHINA ($)

This attractive restaurant with its personable staff is probably the best establishment among the large selection of Chinese restaurants in the Buford Highway corridor. Whole spiced fish, San-Shan soup, homemade noodles and sauce, and several meat and stir-fry vegetable combinations are some of its offerings.
✚ Off map at K1
✉ 5295 Buford Highway
☎ 770/457–6788
🕐 Daily 11:30ᴀᴍ–3ᴀᴍ
🚌 39

HONTO ($)

A favorite of Atlanta's Asian community, this restaurant offers a constantly changing seasonal menu based on authentic Hong Kong-style seafood dishes and other Chinese cuisine. Sampling its *dim sum*, the exotic rolling smorgasbord cart of appetizer-size dishes, is a mouth-watering experience.
✚ Off map at K1
✉ 3295 Chamblee-Dunwoody Road in Chamblee
☎ 770/458–8088
🕐 Sun–Thu 11:30–10; Fri–Sat 11:30–11 🚌 124

KAMOGAWA ($$$)

A very formal Japanese restaurant with a *sushi* bar, regular tables, *teppanyaki* grill tables, and a *tatami* room where you remove your shoes to sit on floor cushions. The excellent food is ceremoniously served. Check out the green-tea ice cream for dessert.
✚ Off map at F1
✉ 3300 Peachtree Road in Hotel Nikko ☎ 404/841–0314
🕐 Daily 11:30–2, 6–10
🚇 Buckhead (N7)
🚌 23, 30, 38

LITTLE SZECHUAN ($)

If you like garlicky Chinese dishes, this is the place for you. Favorites include garlic shrimp, eggplant with garlic, and shredded pork with garlic sauce.
✚ Off map at K1
✉ 5091 Buford Highway in Chamblee ☎ 770/451–0192
🕐 Wed–Mon 11–2, 5–11
🚌 39

SURIN OF THAILAND ($)

Scrumptious, spicy and authentic Thai food. One specialty is a crispy *mee-krob*, a pungent rice-noodle dish with a tamarind sauce garnished with shrimp, eggs, and beansprouts. Check out the exotic drinks such as mango daiquiris.
✚ J4 ✉ 810 North Highland Avenue ☎ 404/892–7789
🕐 Sun–Thu 11:30–10:30; Fri–Sat 11:30–11:30 🚌 16

OTHER INTERNATIONAL RESTAURANTS

COCO LOCO ($)

This small restaurant specializes in Cuban fare. Try the sliced ham with a garlic-cumin-onion-oil marinade, shrimp in garlic sauce, and homemade flan. Set in a strip shopping mall.

➕ Off map at H1
✉ 2625 Piedmont Road (Buckhead Crossing Mall; faces Sidney Marcus Boulevard)
☎ 404/364–0212
🕐 Daily 11–2:30, 6–10
🚇 Lindbergh (N6) 🚌 38, 39

THE DINING ROOM AT THE RITZ-CARLTON ($$$)

This is the top restaurant in the city, a formal dining experience that will put a dent in your budget but won't leave you feeling ripped off. The cuisine is creative and contemporary, the presentations superb, and the service exceptional.

➕ Off map at F1
✉ 3434 Peachtree Road in the Ritz-Carlton Buckhead Hotel
☎ 404/237–2700
🕐 Mon–Sat 6–10
🚇 Buckhead (N7), Lenox (NE7)
🚌 23, 25, 47, 48, 85, 92, 140

FLORENCIA RESTAURANT ($$$)

This elegant restaurant specializes in European dishes with American influences, many based on game. Wild boar chops with baked gnocchi and seared elk chops are favorites, along with rack of lamb and roasted yellow fin tuna.

➕ F3 ✉ 75 14th Street in Occidental Grand Hotel
☎ 404/881–9898
🕐 Tue–Sat 6–11 🚇 Arts Center (N5) 🚌 23, 31, 36, 98

IMPERIAL FEZ ($$)

Resembling a Moroccan prince's tent, this fun restaurant allows you to recline on pillows at low tables and use your fingers to scoop up your meal of good couscous and stewed meats. Belly dancers add to the atmosphere.

➕ Off map at F1 ✉ 2285 Peachtree Road
☎ 404/351–0870 🕐 Daily 6–11 🚌 23

NIKOLAI'S ROOF ($$$)

This elegant 30th-floor restaurant, with a dramatic view of the city, specializes in Russian and classic French cuisine. Reservations are required since the five-course meal is served only twice each night.

➕ G6 ✉ 255 Courtland Street in Atlanta Hilton Hotel
☎ 404/221–6362
🕐 Daily 6:30PM and 9:30PM
🚇 Peachtree Center (N1)
🚌 16, 31, 46

REGGIE'S BRITISH PUB & RESTAURANT ($)

A former Royal Marine has created Atlanta's only truly authentic English pub, serving a good mix of English and American favorites, including seafood chowder, bangers and mash, club sandwiches, and curried chicken.

➕ F6 ✉ 100 Techwood Drive in CNN Center
☎ 404/525–1437 🕐 Daily 11:30–11; open later when events are on at Omni Coliseum
🚇 Omni/Dome/GWCC (W1)
🚌 1, 11, 13, 18, 26, 50, 86

MEXICAN & LATIN RESTAURANTS

Mexican Atlanta

When the oil and construction business declined in Texas a decade ago, Mexicans moved to Atlanta in droves, and the flood hasn't let up yet. To serve their own community, Mexican restaurants sprouted up everywhere, and several offer authentic dishes in settings re-created in the spirit of their homeland. Mexican food is usually good value for the dollar.

CAFÉ TU TU TANGO ($)
Patterned after a Barcelona artist's loft. Strolling artists, musicians and others provide entertainment as you enjoy tasty Spanish *tapas*.
✚ Off map at F1 ✉ 220 Pharr Road ☎ 404/841–6222 ◷ Sun–Wed 11:30AM–midnight; Thu 11:30AM–1AM; Fri–Sat 11:30AM–2AM ▤ 40

DON JUAN'S SPANISH RESTAURANT ($$)
The only place in Atlanta where you can get authentic Spanish (European) cuisine such as paella, chicken Espaniola and *zarzuela* (seafood combination). Five courses are the norm, and there is live entertainment every night.
✚ Off map at H1 ✉ 1927 Piedmont Circle ☎ 404/874–4285 ◷ Mon–Sat 5–11 ▤ 27, 31

EL CHARRO ($)
This lunch-only restaurant offers exceptional authentic Mexican food and drink, including *tacos*, steak, *tortillas*, *margaritas*, and *salsas*.
✚ Off map at H1 ✉ 2581 Piedmont Road in Lindbergh Plaza Shopping Center ☎ 404/264–0613 ◷ 11AM–2:30PM ▣ Lindbergh (N6) ▤ 38, 39

EL TACO VELOZ ($)
Operated by a friendly Mexican family, this restaurant has great beef *tacos*, massive *burritos*, chile *rellenos*, and green *salsa*. *Horchata*, a sweetened rice drink, will help cool your mouth!
✚ Off map at K1 ✉ 5084 Buford Highway

☎ 770/936–9094 ◷ Daily 10AM–9PM ▤ 39

LA PAZ ($)
For spicy Tex-Mex food and a rowdy atmosphere, this is the place. Hearty meat dishes excel, and its *salsas* (spooned on anything served to you) will have you coming back for more. There is also good seafood.
✚ Off map at F1 ✉ 6410 Roswell Road ☎ 404/256–3555 ◷ Sun–Thu 5–10; Fri–Sat 5–11 ▤ 5

RIO BRAVA CANTINA ($)
This is the place to go in Buckhead for Mexican food. Try the *tortilla* sandwiches, *Carne Asade* (a juicy skirt steak topped with green peppers, onions and Monterey Jack cheese), and Mexican sautéed shrimp.
✚ Off map at F1 ✉ 3172 Roswell Road ☎ 404/262–7431 ◷ Daily 11AM–midnight ▤ 38

SUNDOWN CAFÉ ($)
The Sundown offers innovative Mexican and Latin dishes at reasonable prices. Sautéed shrimp cakes, Waco chilli, green chilli stew, and *rancho* mashed potatoes with jalapeño gravy are excellent, and they have 15 versions of *salsa* dip.
✚ Off map at H1 ✉ 2165 Cheshire Bridge Road ☎ 404/231–1118 ◷ Mon–Thu 11–2, 5:30–10; Fri 11–2, 5:30–11; Sat 5:30–11 ▤ 27

ATLANTANS' FAVORITE RESTAURANTS

CITY GRILL ($$)

This posh Downtown restaurant puts an innovative twist on traditional American and southern favorites with barbecue shrimp on grits, cumin-spiced salmon, and chocolate-pecan soufflé pie. Very popular among business people, so expect to wait for a table during lunch hours.

F7 ✉ 50 Hurt Plaza ☎ 404/524–2489 🕐 Mon–Fri 11:30–2:30, 5:30–10; Sat 11:30–2:30, 5:30–2:30AM 🚇 Five Points (0) 🚌 4, 17

DESSERT PLACE ($)

This is the Taj Mahal for Atlanta sweet tooths. Fat cream-cheese brownies, pies, monstrous cakes, coffee concoctions, and much, much more. Yummy.

J3 ✉ 1000 Virginia Avenue ☎ 404/892–8921 🕐 Sun–Thu 9AM–11:30PM; Fri 9AM–1AM; Sat 10AM–1AM 🚌 16, 45

57th FIGHTER GROUP RESTAURANT ($$)

Although the food here is adequate, people tend to come for the ambience. Located alongside the Peachtree-DeKalb Airport runway (you can watch the planes while you eat), it was built to resemble a World War II officers' club complete with sandbagged walls, piped-in songs from the 1940s, and displays of photographs and other artifacts.

Off map at K1 ✉ 3829 Clairmont Road ☎ 770/457–7757 🕐 Sun–Thu 11–2, 5–10; Fri–Sat 11–2, 5–11 🚌 70

INDIGO COASTAL GRILL ($$)

Resembling a chic beach front café, *sans* the ocean view, this is one of the best places for seafood in town, whether it be New England lobsters, cod, and chowder, to lighter favorites reminiscent of the Caribbean. The shrimp dishes and Key lime pie are exceptional.

K2 ✉ 1397 North Highland Avenue ☎ 404/876–0676 🕐 Daily 5:30–11 🚌 16

PANO AND PAULS ($$$)

The intimate and elegant setting of this restaurant, combined with its often innovative menu, will make a return customer of you. The food will captivate you, from caviar with oysters and steak in herb sauce to the eggplant terrine.

Off map at F1 ✉ 1232 West Paces Ferry Road ☎ 404/261–3662 🕐 Mon–Fri 6–10; Sat 6–11 🚌 40, 58

SUN DIAL RESTAURANT & LOUNGE ($$)

Come here for the view, if not the food. On a clear day the panoramic views from this revolving bar and restaurant atop the 73-story-high Westin Peachtree Plaza Hotel stretch over the entire city and far beyond. At night it's awesome to see all the buildings lit up.

F6 ✉ 210 Peachtree Street in Westin Peachtree Plaza Hotel ☎ 404/589–7506 🕐 Daily 11–2:30, 5:30–11 🚇 Peachtree Center (N1) 🚌 10, 13, 31

SHOPPING MALLS

Mall capital of America

No other city in the United States, Chicago excepted, can compete with Atlanta when it comes to mall shopping space. You'll see why indoor shopping is so popular if you arrive during the summer, when outside conditions can be torrid.

LENOX SQUARE MALL

The largest shopping mall in the Southeast, with 268 shops. It has a broad mix, with the Macy's, Rich's and Neiman Marcus department stores, several popular chain stores, and specialty retailers such as Godiva Chocolatier. There is also a food court, a movie theater complex, and several restaurants.
✚ Off map at H1 ✉ 3393 Peachtree Road at Lenox Road ☎ 404/233–6767; 800/344–5222 🕐 Mon–Sat 10–9:30; Sun 12:30–5:30 🚇 Buckhead (N7), Lenox (NE7) 🚌 23, 25, 47, 48, 85, 92, 140

THE MALL AT PEACHTREE CENTER

Beneath and at the rear of a fountained, open-air plaza surrounded by four corner-office towers are over 80 shops, restaurants, and services, including a food court with a dozen fast-food outlets.
✚ F6 ✉ 225 Peachtree Street ☎ 404/614–5000 🕐 Mon–Sat 10–6; Sun noon–5:30, but can vary 🚇 Peachtree Center (N1) 🚌 10, 13, 31

NORTH POINT MALL

With six department stores, this is the largest mall on the north side of metropolitan Atlanta. It has interesting specialty stores including Atlanta Brave's Clubhouse, Euro Art, Great Train, Smart Stuf, and Ozone Hi-Tech.
✚ Off map at G1 ✉ 1000 North Point Circle (off GA 400) in Alpharetta ☎ 770/740–9273 🕐 Mon–Sat 10–9:30; Sun noon–6 🚌 140 from Lenox (NE7) to Mansell Road "Park & Ride" lot, then transfer to 141

NORTHLAKE MALL

Northlake includes Macy's, J. C. Penney, Sears Roebuck, and the upscale Parisian department stores, a food court and a couple of restaurants. Located in northeast Atlanta.
✚ Off map at K1 ✉ 4800 Briarcliff Road ☎ 404/938–3564 🕐 Mon–Sat 10–9:30; Sun 12:30–5:30 🚌 30, 91, 125

PERIMETER MALL

This mall, located about 15 minutes' drive north of Lenox Square Mall in the affluent suburb of Dunwoody, is known for quality family shopping. Here you will find the High Museum of Art Gift Shop, Gap Kids, and The Nature Company, as well as Macy's and Rich's department stores.
✚ Off map at K1 ✉ 4400 Ashford-Dunwoody Road at I-285 ☎ 770/394–4270 🕐 Mon–Sat 10–9; Sun 12:30–5:30 🚇 Dunwoody (N9) 🚌 150

PHIPPS PLAZA

This three-level, 200-store mall caters to wealthy shoppers, with Saks Fifth Avenue, Bloomingdales, Lord & Taylor, Gucci, Parisian, Tiffany & Co., Abercrombie & Fitch, and several smaller specialty shops. It also has a movie theater complex, a food court and a number of restaurants.
✚ Off map at K1 ✉ 3500 Peachtree Road at Lenox Road ☎ 404/262–0992 🕐 Mon–Sat 10–9; Sun noon–5:30 🚇 Buckhead (N7), Lenox (NE7) 🚌 23, 25, 47, 48, 85, 92, 140

DEPARTMENT STORES

J. C. PENNEY
This long-established chain caters to the needs of the middle class with affordable clothes and hard-wearing furniture.
Off map at K1 ✉ Northlake Mall, 4800 Briarcliff Road; also at five other malls ☎ 404/434–2561; 800/222–6161 🕙 Mon–Sat 10–9:30; Sun 12:30–6 🚌 30, 91, 125

MACY'S
The Downtown location of this department store— housed in a six-story, Italian villa-style building—first opened for business as Davisons department store in 1927. Offering a broad range of goods, with especially good clothing, gourmet foods and kitchen accessory departments, it is the last of the grand department stores (chandeliers, marble floors and high ceilings) left in Atlanta that isn't connected to a mall.
F6 ✉ 180 Peachtree Street; also at eight malls ☎ 404/221–7221; 800/456–2297 🕙 Mon–Sat 10–6; Sun noon–6 🚇 Peachtree Center (N1) 🚌 10, 13, 16, 31

NEIMAN MARCUS
This famed department store caters to the upper class and has been a mainstay of Lenox Square Mall for over two decades. Even if you don't have the money, the merchandise is fun to look at—especially during the Christmas season. Precious jewelry, perfume, and designer-label clothing departments are its trademark.
Off map at K1 ✉ Lenox Square Mall, 3393 Peachtree Road at Lenox Road ☎ 404/266–8200 🕙 Mon–Sat 10–9:30; Sun 12:30–5:30 🚇 Buckhead (N7), Lenox (NE7) 🚌 23, 25, 47, 48, 85, 92, 140

PARISIAN
This chain store has extremely helpful staff, and offers classic and semi-upscale goods to a wide clientele. Its recent entry into the Atlanta market brings a bit of class to the mall scene.
Off map at K1 ✉ Phipps Plaza, 3500 Peachtree Road at Lenox Road; also at three other malls ☎ 404/814–3200 🕙 Mon–Sat 10–9; Sun noon–5:30 🚇 Buckhead (N7), Lenox (NE7) 🚌 23, 25, 47, 48, 85, 92, 140

RICH'S
Rich's is considered the city's best department store chain, with well-planned shops and a variety of goods at prices slightly lower than Macy's.
Off map at K1 ✉ Lenox Square Mall, 3393 Peachtree Road at Lenox Road; also at 11 other malls ☎ 800/282–8800 🕙 Mon–Sat 10–9:30; Sun 12:30–6 🚇 Buckhead (N7), Lenox (NE7) 🚌 23, 25, 47, 48, 85, 92, 140

SAKS FIFTH AVENUE
A branch of the famous high-fashion department store brings New York sophistication to Atlanta. Buy designer clothes, shoes, furs and perfumes.
Off map at K1 ✉ Phipps Plaza, 3500 Peachtree Road at Lenox Road ☎ 404/261–7234 🕙 Mon–Fri 10–9; Sat 10–7; Sun 12:30–5:30 🚇 Buckhead (N7), Lenox (NE7) 🚌 23, 25, 47, 48, 85, 92, 140

Shopping paradise
If you ask visitors from other southern locations why they come to Atlanta, the answer will probably be: 1) to visit relatives; 2) to attend a convention; 3) sports; 4) entertainment; or 5) shopping (the latter is ranked number 1 among women). Atlanta is a mecca for shoppers: if you can't find it here, it won't be anywhere else in the South.

71

ANTIQUES SHOPS & DISTRICTS

Antiques galore

You can "shop till you drop" and still not hit all the antiques shops in Atlanta. Although the greatest concentration of them is in the sprawling Buckhead neighborhood and suburban Chamblee, consider renting a car to venture to the outer suburbs of Roswell, Norcross and Buford, where you will find several outstanding shops.

ATLANTA ANTIQUE CENTER AND FLEA MARKET

In this 80,000-square foot warehouse setting are 150 dealers selling antique furniture and decorative items (primarily American and English), collectibles, glassware and other items.

➕ Off map at K1 ✉ 5360 Peachtree Industrial Boulevard in Chamblee ☎ 770/458–0456 🕐 Fri–Sat 11–7; Sun noon–7 🚇 Chamblee (N9) 🚌 25

BENNETT STREET GALLERIES

This former street of warehouses now contains over 150 art galleries, and antiques shops. The Stalls (116 Bennett Street) features 75 antiques and decorative art furnishings dealers; another 45 dealers are in the Interiors Market (55 Bennett Street). It's a fun place for buying and browsing.

➕ Off map at F1 ✉ Bennett Street off Peachtree Road (2100 block) 🕐 Daily 9–6 (some shops have later hours) 🚌 23

CHAMBLEE'S ANTIQUE ROW

Over 200 antiques and collectibles dealers are housed here in historic 19th-century homes, shops and former churches along Broad Street and Peachtree Road in suburban Chamblee. Whatever you are looking for—and 19th- and early 20th-century furniture and knickknacks in particular—will probably be found here.

➕ Off map at K1 ✉ Broad Street at Peachtree Road 🕐 Mon–Sat 10:30–5; Sun 1–5 for most shops 🚇 Chamblee (NE9) 🚌 129, 132

MIAMI CIRCLE

On the fringe of Buckhead is a street lined with over 34 high-quality antiques and decorative arts dealers. Le Primitif Gallery (631 Miami Circle), specializing in antiques from Haiti, is interesting, while Williams Antiques (631-B Miami Circle) is Georgia's oldest antiques business.

➕ Off map at H1 ✉ Miami Circle, off Piedmont Road about 2 miles from I-85 🕐 Mon–Sat 10–6; Sun noon–5, although times vary 🚇 Lindbergh (N6) 🚌 38, 39

20TH CENTURY ANTIQUES

This shop, located in the popular Virginia-Highland business district, has an eclectic combination of antique objects, including old furniture, radios, southwestern accent pieces, silver mirrors, art deco items, and Limoges plates.

➕ J3 ✉ 1044 North Highland Avenue ☎ 404/892–2065 🕐 Mon–Wed 1–7; Thu–Sat 11–9; Sun noon–6 🚌 16, 45

THE WRECKING BAR

Housed in a National Register, 19th-century home near the Little Five Points business district, this antiques shop has 18,000 square feet of architectural antiques, including doors, mantels, light fixtures, stained-glass windows, porch pedestals, and hardware.

➕ K6 ✉ 292 Moreland Avenue ☎ 404/525–0468 🕐 Mon–Sat 9–5 🚇 Inman Park–Reynoldstown (E3) 🚌 3, 48

ART & SOUTHERN HANDICRAFTS GALLERIES

ALIYA–THE GALLERY OF MORNINGSIDE

This gallery represents 30 of the region's hottest artists in painting, sculpture, glass, and mixed media. This is exceptional work by the next generation of great artists, so buy it while it is still affordable.

✚ K2 ✉ 1402 North Highland Avenue, Suite 4
☎ 404/892–2835
🕐 Tue–Sun 11–10 🚌 16

BERMAN GALLERY

Specializing in ceramics, paintings and other creations by southern craftspeople such as Minnie Evans, this was the first gallery in Atlanta to show the religious-oriented folk paintings of Howard Finster, a former Georgia preacher and now an internationally recognized artist. Finster has designed album covers for the rock bands Adam Again, REM, and Talking Heads.

✚ Off map at F1
✉ 3261 Roswell Road
☎ 404/261–3858
🕐 Tue–Sat 10–5 🚌 38

FAY GOLD GALLERY

Fay Gold is noted for her cutting-edge shows of nationally and internationally renowned contemporary artists, photographers and sculptors. The works exhibited here are usually modern and often controversial, such as the photographs of Robert Mapplethorpe.

✚ Off map at F1
✉ 247 Buckhead Avenue
☎ 404/233–3843
🕐 Mon–Sat 9:30–5:30 🚌 23, 38, 40

FORM AND FUNCTION GALLERY

Instead of art that you hang on your wall, this gallery specializes in functional pieces with an artsy bent. Chairs, tables, lamps, bowls and other familiar objects appear in creative and whimsical forms—for example, the gallery has displayed a set of chairs created from car gas tanks.

✚ J4 ✉ 784 North Highland Avenue, Suite 5
☎ 404/892–3193
🕐 Thu–Sat noon–10; Tue, Sun noon–6; Wed noon–7 🚌 16

JACKSON FINE ART GALLERY

This is the best place to purchase photography by world-renowned 20th-century American and European photographers such as Ansel Adams, Walker Evans, Bill Brandt, Henri Cartier-Bresson, Robert Doisneau, Edward Weston, and others.

✚ Off map at F1 ✉ 3115 East Shadowlawn Avenue
☎ 404/233–3739
🕐 Mon–Fri 9–6; Sat 10:30–5:30 🚌 23, 40

SIGNATURE SHOP AND GALLERY

This is the oldest crafts-only gallery in the country, with handmade artistic and functional works created from fiber, clay, metal, wood, glass, and paper by both regional and nationally recognized craftspeople.

✚ Off map at F1
✉ 3267 Roswell Road
☎ 404/237–4426
🕐 Mon–Sat 10–5 🚌 38

Naturally crafty

The Southern Appalachian region, of which Atlanta is geographically a part, has a long history of craftspeople producing artistic and functional pieces from available natural products. With an abundance of clay and forests, Georgia has some of the nation's best potters and woodworkers. When you are gallery hopping, make sure you include stops at those galleries that specialize in crafts.

BOOKSTORES

ARCHITECTURAL BOOK CENTER

This small bookshop, run by the American Institute of Architects (AIA), has books about architecture in Atlanta and other world locations, travel guides and a few art books. It also has an interesting selection of greeting cards, T-shirts, and unusual gifts.

🚹 F6 ✉ The Mall at Peachtree Center (➤ 70)
☎ 404/222–9920
🕐 Mon–Sat 10–6
🚇 Peachtree Center (N1)
🚌 10, 13, 31

THE BOOK NOOK

This is the largest secondhand bookshop in Atlanta, with over 200,000 titles priced at 60 percent of the original retail price. It also sells secondhand music cassette tapes, CDs, record albums, comic books, current magazines, and some books.

🚹 Off map at K1
✉ 3342 Clairmont Road
☎ 404/633–1328 🕐 Daily 10–11 🚌 19, 39, 70

BORDERS BOOKS AND MUSIC SHOP

Borders' large new shop boasts 120,000 book titles, 60,000 CDs and cassettes, 8,000 music videos, and a café.

🚹 Off map at K1
✉ 3637 Peachtree Road, N.E.
☎ 404/237–0707
🕐 Mon–Sat 9–9; Sun 11–6
🚌 25, 85, 92, 140

CHARIS BOOKS

This long-established Little Five Points bookshop specializes in feminist books, cassettes, cards, T-shirts, and more. It holds special programs every Thursday night at 7:30PM.

🚹 K5 ✉ 1189 Euclid Avenue
☎ 404/524–0304
🕐 Mon–Tue, Thu 10:30–6:30; Wed 10:30–8; Fri–Sat 10:30–10; Sun noon–6 🚇 Inman Park–Reynoldstown (E3)
🚌 3, 48

OXFORD BOOKS

Oxford is the largest independent bookstore in the Southeast. Its main Atlanta store features weekly book signings by famous authors, and also has a large section of magazines and newspapers (including some from Europe), a rare books and collectibles section, and a video department. It also sells sheet music, tapes and CDs, and exhibits local artists' work. Its Espresso Café serves light meals, coffee, beverages, and desserts.

🚹 Off map at F1
✉ 360 Pharr Road; also at two other locations
☎ 404/262–3333
🕐 Sun–Thu 9AM–midnight; Fri–Sat 9AM–2AM
🚌 23, 38, 40

TALL TALES

This small shop, run by a very knowledgable staff, excels in regional fiction and travel books. There's a small coffee bar.

🚹 Off map at K1
✉ 2999 North Druid Hills Road in Toco Hills Shopping Center ☎ 404/636–2498
🕐 Mon–Sat 10:30–9; Sun 12:30–6:30 🚌 8, 30

MEN'S CLOTHING

BENNIE'S DISCOUNT SHOES

When Atlantan men need fine dress or casual shoes, they head for Bennie's. All major brand names are discounted on the store's bargain tables, some by as much as 75 percent.
➕ Off map at H1 ✉ 2581 Piedmont Road in Lindbergh Plaza Shopping Center
☎ 404/262–1966
🕐 Mon–Sat 8–6 🚇 Lindbergh (N6) 🚌 38, 39

BROOKS BROTHERS

America's oldest clothing company (established in 1818) has high-quality men's wear in traditional cuts and fabrics. Good selection of suits, shirts, and ties.
➕ F6 ✉ The Mall at Peachtree Center and Lenox Square Mall (➤ 70) ☎ 404/577–4040
🕐 Mon–Sat 10–6 🚇 Peachtree Center (N1), Lenox (NE7)
🚌 10, 13, 31

FRIEDMAN'S SHOES

Friedman's sells shoes in sizes ranging from 7 to 20 (width A–EEE); it became popular after professional athletes began telling their teammates and friends about it—now it attracts visiting team buses. Autographed balls, shirts, and photographs are displayed.
➕ F7 ✉ 209 Mitchell Street; also at two other locations
☎ 404/524–1311
🕐 Mon–Sat 9–5:30 🚇 Five Points (0) 🚌 1

GENTLY OWNED

This men's store specializes in upscale designer clothing at discount prices. Fifty percent of the clothes come from European buyouts, the other half being slightly used garments.
➕ Off map at F1 ✉ 3209 Paces Ferry Place
☎ 404/262–1881 🕐 Mon noon–6; Tue–Sat 10:30–8; Sun 9:30–6 🚌 23, 40, 58

INTERNATIONAL MAN

Sophisticated and fashionable clothes by Canali, Pancaldi, Moschino, Gianfranco Ferre, and others.
➕ Off map at K1 ✉ Phipps Plaza (➤ 70)
☎ 404/841–0770
🕐 Mon–Sat 10–9; Sun noon–5:30 🚇 Buckhead (N7), Lenox (NE7) 🚌 23, 25, 47, 48, 85, 92, 140

THE MEN'S WEARHOUSE OUTLET STORE

This is one of three nationwide clearance shops for this national men's clothing chain. Thousands of designer suits, shirts, ties, and accessories are discounted. Suits can be bought for less than $200, and shirts and ties for less than $15.
➕ C1 ✉ 1218 Old Chattahoochee Avenue ☎ 404/351–1060 🕐 Mon–Sat 10–7; Sun noon–6 🚌 1

SEBASTIAN'S CLOSET

The top men's clothing fashions are sold here, including clothes by the designers Hugo Boss, Pal Zileri, Vestimenta, Zanella, Jhane Barnes, and Donna Karan.
➕ Off map at F1 ✉ 3222 Peachtree Road
☎ 404/365–9033
🕐 Mon–Sat 10–6; Thu until 8
🚌 23

WOMEN'S CLOTHING

Vintage and retro to go

Vintage and retro clothes are in. To find them, check out Little Five Points: most notably Stefan's Vintage Clothing (✉ 1160 Euclid Avenue), The Junkman's Daughter (✉ 1130 Euclid Avenue), and Pink Flamingos (✉ 1166 Euclid Avenue). Other good sources are consignment shops and thrift shops throughout the city.

AJS SHOE WAREHOUSE

This is the best place for women's shoes, with major brand names available at great discounts.

➕ C3 ✉ 1788 Ellsworth Industrial Boulevard
☎ 404/355–1760
🕐 Fri–Sat 10–6 🚍 1

BACKSTREET BOUTIQUE

This is Buckhead's quality resale consignment shop, where you can look like a million dollars for a fraction of the price. Adolfo, Chanel, and Donna Karan are among the brands you find here.

➕ Off map at F1
✉ 3655 Roswell Road
☎ 404/262–7783
🕐 Tue–Fri 11–6; Sat 10–5
🚍 23, 38

CHEZ JACKI

Upscale and fashionable clothing for career-minded women. Great selection of evening dresses and gowns, plus classy accessories.

➕ F6 ✉ The Mall at Peachtree Center (➤ 70)
☎ 404/523–1325
🕐 Mon–Sat 10–6
🚇 Peachtree Center (N1)
🚍 10, 13, 31

MITZI & ROMANO

This shop sells cutting-edge American and European clothes, jewelry, and accessories from designers such as Kenar, French Connection, and Betsey Johnson.

➕ J3 ✉ 1038 North Highland Avenue ☎ 404/876–7228
🕐 Mon 11–8; Tue–Thu 11–9; Fri–Sat 11–10; Sun noon–7
🚍 16, 45

RENÉ RENÉ

These shops are a showcase for the creations of local fashion designer René Sanning, known for her avant-garde and original designs with a combination modern/1940s retro look, including interesting accessories.

➕ F2 ✉ 1776 Peachtree Street ☎ 404/875–7883
🚇 Arts Center (N5) 🚍 16, 23.
➕ K5 ✉ 1142 Euclid Avenue in Little Five Points (➤ 18)
☎ 404/522–RENE 🚇 Inman Park–Reynoldstown (E3) 🚍 48
🕐 Mon–Fri 11:30–6:30; Sat 11–7; Sun 1–5

REXER-PARKES

This classy shop sells fashionable clothes for women who wear junior sizes. When you need a little black dress or a complete wardrobe for the office, this is the place. Good selection of weekend casual wear, lingerie, and accessories too.

➕ Off map at F1
✉ 2140 Peachtree Road in Brookwood Square Shopping Center ☎ 404/351–3080
🕐 Mon–Wed, Fri 10–7; Thu 10–9; Sat 10–6 🚍 23

STONE MOUNTAIN HANDBAG FACTORY STORE

This company is known throughout the South for its high-quality leather handbags and purses at 20–50 percent off the retail price.

➕ Off map at K4 ✉ 963 Main Street in Stone Mountain
☎ 770/498–1316
🕐 Mon–Sat 10–6; Sun 1–5
🚍 118, 120

FINE GIFTS & SOUVENIRS

ARTLITE

Although primarily an office supply shop, Artlite has the best selection of pens in Atlanta, including major brands such as Mont Blanc, Parker, Colibri, Visconti, Waterman, Cross, Lamy, and Sheaffer.

✚ H1 ✉ 1851 Piedmont Road
☎ 404/875–7271
🕐 Mon–Fri 8–6; Sat 9–5
🚌 31

CITY ART WORKS

This shop sells uniquely designed crafts that emphasize function as well as design. There's furniture, dinnerware, tabletop items for the home and office, jewelry, mirrors, picture frames, candle holders, and decorative objects.

✚ Off map at F1 ✉ 2140 Peachtree Road in Brookwood Square Shopping Center
☎ 404/605–0786
🕐 Mon–Wed, Sat 10–6:30; Thu–Fri 10–8 🚌 23

GIFTS EXTRAORDINAIRE

Looking more like an art gallery, this small gift shop sells a wide array of interestingly designed decorative objects, including crafted metal creations and wall sculptures, mobiles, raku pottery, and candles.

✚ Off map at K1
✉ Phipps Plaza (➤ 70)
☎ 404/365–9231
🕐 Mon–Sat 10–9; Sun noon–5:30 🚇 Buckhead (N7), Lenox (NE7) 🚌 23, 25, 47, 48, 85, 92, 140

MUSEUM SHOP

This store has fine-art books, jewelry, prints, games, clothes, and other items from the gift shops of some of America's best museums all under one roof.

✚ Off map at K1
✉ Phipps Plaza (➤ 70)
☎ 404/365–8019
🕐 Mon–Sat 10–9:30; Sun 12:30–5:30 🚇 Buckhead (N7), Lenox (NE7) 🚌 23, 25, 47, 48, 85, 92, 140

THE SHARPER IMAGE

This San Francisco chain offers an eclectic group of gift-oriented items ranging from clothes, shoes and jewelry to sophisticated electronic calculators and language converters. It also sells health-oriented products such as massagers and exercise equipment, and a variety of sophisticated toys.

✚ Off map at K1 ✉ Lenox Square Mall (➤ 70)
☎ 404/261–8388
🕐 Mon–Sat 10–9:30; Sun 12:30–5:30 🚇 Buckhead (N7), Lenox (NE7) 🚌 23, 25, 47, 48, 85, 92, 140

A TOUCH OF GEORGIA

This is the place to buy Georgia theme T-shirts and coffee mugs with a peach (a state emblem) or state map printed on them, plus numerous edible products such as Muscadine jelly and peach butter created from fruits grown in Georgia.

✚ F6 ✉ The Mall at Peachtree Center (➤ 70)
☎ 404/577–6681
🕐 Mon–Sat 10–6
🚇 Peachtree Center (N1)
🚌 10, 13, 31

Sports gifts

Being a professional sports town, Atlanta is home to several stores like the Brave's Clubhouse (CNN Center), where you can buy authentic shirts, uniforms, caps, T-shirts, and other novelty items representing the home teams.

HALLS & ARENAS

Buying tickets

The cost of living in the South as a whole is often cheaper than the rest of the nation—but not Atlanta entertainment. For national acts you'll pay more or less what you would anywhere else. You can get tickets at on-site box offices or from TicketMaster (☎ 404/249–6400 or 800/326–4000). Consult the Atlanta Journal & Constitution's Friday "Weekend Preview" or Saturday "Leisure" tabloid sections about forthcoming events (➤ 92).

ATLANTA CIVIC CENTER

With its large stage, this is a favorite venue of theater companies and other groups who need a lot of space. With no obstructing pillars, this concert hall has good sight lines.
➕ G5 ✉ 395 Piedmont Avenue ☎ 404/523–6275 🚇 Civic Center (N2) 🚌 16, 46

CHASTAIN PARK AMPHITHEATER

Many Atlantans look forward to Chastain's summer concert series, which offers music ranging from the Atlanta Symphony Orchestra to blues rocker Bonnie Raitt, country star Willie Nelson, and New Age musician Yanni. Several levels of seating are available, from tables where you can dine to the lawn (bring a blanket).
➕ Off map at F1 ✉ 4469 Stella Drive ☎ Tickets: 404/733–5000. Concert information: 404/233–7275 🚌 38

COCA-COLA LAKEWOOD AMPHITHEATER

From May to the end of October, rock music concerts are held at this outdoor amphitheater, which can accommodate 18,000 people. The Allman Brothers, Rod Stewart, Eric Clapton, and other popular acts have performed here.
➕ E/F13 ✉ 2002 Lakewood Way ☎ 404/627–5700 🚌 Shuttle bus from Lakewood–Fort McPherson station (S4), or 17, 100

FOX THEATRE

For many Atlantans, this is the number one place to view entertainment (➤ 41). With only 4,518 seats, it is intimate, and the acoustics are good. A regular schedule of popular music groups from Bob Dylan to the Rolling Stones play here; large touring Broadway theater productions such as Annie, Cats, and Les Misérables offer regular performances; and there is an annual summer film festival.
➕ F4 ✉ 660 Peachtree Street ☎ 404/881–2100 🚇 North Avenue (N3) 🚌 2, 10, 45

GEORGIA DOME

The Atlanta Falcons (➤ 83) host other NFL teams in this mammoth enclosed stadium (seats 70,500 people) eight Sundays annually. During the rest of the year it is used for a variety of events ranging from motorcycle racing and concerts to conventions.
➕ E6 ✉ 1 Georgia Dome Drive ☎ 404/223–9200 🚇 Omni/Dome/GWCC (W1) 🚌 1, 11, 13, 18, 26, 50, 86

OMNI COLISEUM

This is the home of Atlanta's professional basketball team, the Hawks. The 16,000-seat venue is also used for large rock concerts, conventions, ice-skating shows, and the circus.
➕ E6 ✉ 100 Techwood Drive behind CNN Center ☎ 404/681–2100 🚇 Omni/Dome/ GWCC (W1) 🚌 1, 11, 13, 18, 26, 50, 86

THEATERS

ACADEMY THEATRE

Atlanta's oldest theater company (since 1956) and the second-oldest resident company in the United States performs original works by local and contemporary playwrights about modern themes and social problems.

✚ E5 ▨ 501 Means Avenue
☎ 404/525–4111
🚌 1, 26, 50

ACTOR'S EXPRESS

This critically acclaimed theater company is housed in a renovated factory warehouse, and presents cutting-edge and eclectic productions by local and nationally renowned playwrights about modern themes and issues.

✚ E5 ▨ 887 West Marietta Street in King Plow Arts Center
☎ 404/875–1606
🚌 1, 11, 26, 50

ALLIANCE THEATRE

Considered one of the South's best professional theater companies, the Alliance performs everything from Shakespeare and Dickens' *A Christmas Carol* to the latest Broadway shows.

✚ F3 ▨ 1280 Peachtree Street (Woodruff Arts Center)
☎ 404/733–5000 🚇 Arts Center (N5) 🚌 10, 23, 35, 36, 48, 98

NEIGHBORHOOD PLAYHOUSE

This is perhaps the best community theater in the Atlanta area, staging mainstream dramas, comedies, and musicals in a 160-seat auditorium in a former elementary school.

✚ Off map at K5 ▨ 430 West Trinity Place (Decatur)
☎ 404/373–5311 🚇 Decatur (E6) 🚌 15, 17, 96

ONSTAGE ATLANTA & ABRACADABRA! CHILDREN'S THEATRE

This long-established theater group offers a consistently interesting season of drama, comedies and musicals from its intimate theater. In the same location, the ABRACADABRA! Children's Theatre performs original plays and stage adaptations of works such as *Charlotte's Web* and *Winnie the Pooh*.

✚ G5 ▨ 420 Courtland Street
☎ 404/897–1802
🚇 Peachtree Center (N1), Civic Center (N2) 🚌 16, 46

7 STAGES THEATER

Works by contemporary playwrights performed here are usually thought-provoking or controversial, covering a variety of social topics and taboos from racism to the homeless to homosexuality.

✚ J6 ▨ 1105 Euclid Avenue
☎ 404/523–7647 🚇 Inman Park–Reynoldstown (E3)
🚌 3, 48

STAGE DOOR PLAYERS

An established non-profit theater a short distance north of I-285 in suburban Dunwoody. Professional, amateur, and student talent perform classic and contemporary works.

✚ Off map at K1
▨ 5339 Chamblee–Dunwoody Road (Dunwoody)
☎ 404/396–1726
♿ Accessible only by car or taxi

Homegrown talent

Although not world-renowned for its theater companies, Atlanta is a proving ground for actors, actresses, and playwrights who go on to bigger things in other cities. Many fall in love with the city, and prefer not to leave despite their great talent. You may not recognize their names on the posters, but you are guaranteed of receiving good and innovative theater.

CLASSICAL MUSIC & DANCE

Music from the colleges

Outside the professional realm, one of the best places to hear classical music at very affordable prices is from the various orchestras and choral groups connected to the 30-odd colleges and universities in the area. The Emory University brass, chamber, and wind ensembles are quite good (☎ 404/727–6187); alternatively, look for concerts by the University Symphony (☎ 404/651–3676), composed of members of several Atlanta colleges.

MUSIC

ATLANTA BOYS' CHOIR

This choir of 175 boys aged 5–14, modeled on the Vienna Boys' Choir, has been delighting international audiences since it started performing in 1956. The Grammy Award-winning group performs frequently in Atlanta and goes on an annual tour of Mexico and Europe. Its concerts in local churches are highlights of the Christmas season.

⊠ Various venues
☎ 404/378–0064

ATLANTA OPERA ASSOCIATION

This association of local singers and musicians, augmented by international artists, performs three to five times a year, with a repertoire including everything from the classics to more modern themes. The productions look and sound very professional, often getting good reviews. To help the audience, a screen placed above the stage displays a translation of the text.

✚ F3 ⊠ Usually at Symphony Hall (see below)
☎ 404/355–3311 Arts Center (N5) 10, 23, 35, 36, 48, 98

ATLANTA SYMPHONY ORCHESTRA

This world-class and award-winning symphony orchestra, under the musical direction of Yoel Levi, recently celebrated its 50th anniversary. It performs its fall–spring Master Season subscription series in the 1,800-seat Symphony Hall and has a Summer Pops Concert series outdoors at the Chastain Park Amphitheater (➤ 78). It also performs at other city locations for special events.

✚ F3 ⊠ 1280 Peachtree Street (Woodruff Arts Center)
☎ 404/733–5000 Arts Center (N5) 10, 23, 35, 36, 48, 98

DANCE

THE ATLANTA BALLET COMPANY

The nation's oldest continually operating professional ballet company (founded in 1929) consistently receives international recognition for its high-quality productions of classical and contemporary works. Its annual rendition of Tchaikovsky's *Nutcracker* is outstanding. Ticket prices, although generally expensive, are greatly discounted one hour before curtain time.

✚ G5 ⊠ Usually at the Atlanta Civic Center (➤ 78)
☎ 404/892–3303 Civic Center (N2) 16, 46

INTERNATIONAL BALLET ROTARU

Romanian Pavel Rotaru, who spent a year with the Atlanta Ballet, leads this troupe with a series of classical and colorful ballet performances. They are a good alternative if the Atlanta Ballet is not in town.

✚ F4 ⊠ Usually at the Fox Theatre (➤ 41)
☎ 770/395–5322 North Avenue (N3) 2, 10, 45

MUSIC CLUBS

Please note: The hours given for the clubs listed below are starting times for musical entertainment up to closing time. Those clubs that serve food and drink open earlier, so call in advance for their hours if you want to dine there. Establishments with live entertainment usually have a cover charge and/or minimum drink charge.

BLIND WILLIE'S

This is the best blues parlor in town for both music and atmosphere. Small, smoky, and always crowded, it features vocalists and bands playing Mississippi Delta and New Orleans-style blues—both vocal and instrumental pieces. Local musicians, rising stars and legendary greats can all be found here. Unless you want to listen from outside, try to get here early.

⬛ J4 ✉ 828 North Highland Avenue ☎ 404/873–2583 🕐 Daily 8PM–2AM 🚌 16

CHAMELEON CLUB

This Buckhead club is a frequent haunt of the under-30s, who come to hear new alternative and progressive rock bands, as well as the blues featured on Wednesday nights. Dress is very casual, and there's a dance floor.

⬛ Off map at F1 ✉ 3179 Peachtree Road ☎ 404/261–8004 🕐 Daily 11PM–4AM 🚌 23

DANTE'S DOWN THE HATCH

This jazz music club has been a favorite of locals and tourists alike for more than 20 years. You enter it through a streetside hatchway reminiscent of an old pirate ship. You then descend to the lower decks, where the nautical theme is continued with a ship's steering wheel, a wharf front where the musicians play, and a moat with three live crocodiles.

⬛ F7 ✉ Kenny's Alley in Underground Atlanta (▶ 29) ☎ 404/577–1800 🕐 Mon–Thu 5PM–midnight; Fri–Sat 5PM–1AM; Sun 5PM–11PM 🚇 Five Points (0) 🚌 3, 13, 17, 20, 42, 90, 97

EDDIE'S ATTIC

This upstairs club is the best place to hear local and national acoustic acts. Seating 225 people, it was one of the first gigs for the now famous Indigo Girls duo. The shows start early; it's an "all ages, no smoking" concert, and parents are allowed to bring their children to the club.

⬛ Off map at K4 ✉ 515-B North McDonough Street in Decatur ☎ 404/377–4976 🕐 Daily; shows at 7PM and 9:30PM 🚇 Decatur (E6) 🚌 15, 17, 18, 96

THE POINT

This small club, located in Little Five Points, is a showcase for up-and-coming rock, reggae, and progressive music groups.

⬛ K5 ✉ 420 Moreland Avenue ☎ 404/659–3522 🕐 Daily 10PM–2AM 🚇 Inman Park–Reynoldstown (E3) 🚌 3, 48

Music, music, music

Atlanta has one of the best music club scenes in the nation, with blues, country, folk, jazz, and every form of rock music heard in bars and clubs throughout the city and beyond to the suburbs. Where it excels most is in acoustic music and alternative-progressive rock fashioned after the famed REM, who began their career at the University of Georgia.

DANCE CLUBS

Hotlanta

Atlanta, nicknamed "Hotlanta" by the city's party animals, is the undisputed entertainment capital of the South. Its varied nightlife scene has something for all ages, especially the 25–40 group, which makes up a large percentage of the population. Following their lead, begin with a meal at a chic restaurant, take in a concert or show at a music club, and finish by dancing the early morning away.

BACKSTREET

The mainstay of the gay club scene for 20 years. Dancing begins at 10PM, and there's a female impersonator show every Friday and Saturday night.

➕ G4 ✉ 845 Peachtree Street ☎ 404/873–1986 ⏲ Daily 10PM–2AM 🚇 Midtown (N4) 🚌 10, 31

BUCKBOARD COUNTRY MUSIC SHOWCASE

This is the largest country music dance club in metro Atlanta. Its house band pumps out the latest country rhythms, and there's lots of two-stepping country line-dancing. Occasional celebrities pop in for Thursday night showcases.

➕ Off map at C1 ✉ 2080 Cobb Parkway in Windy Hill Plaza Shopping Center ☎ 770/955–7340 ⏲ Mon–Fri 9PM–2AM; Sat 9PM–3AM ♿ Accessible only by car or taxi

CITY LIGHTS

This no-smoking, alcohol-free dance hall in suburban Doraville features ballroom dancing to the tempestuous tango. Regulars range in age from 20 to 50.

➕ Off map at K1 ✉ 5841 Buford Highway ☎ 404/451/5461 ⏲ Mon–Sat 8PM–1AM 🚇 Doraville (NE10) 🚌 39, 91, 124

CLUB ANYTIME

When the other clubs close, Atlantans come here for dancing to pop music spun by a DJ.

➕ G3 ✉ 1055 Peachtree Street ☎ 404/607–8050 ⏲ Daily 24 hours 🚇 Midtown (N4) 🚌 10

JOHNNY'S HIDEAWAY

This is one of the most popular dance clubs in Atlanta for the over-40 set. Open every evening, it features everything from ballroom dancing to the big-band sounds of the 1940s–1950s, Presley ballads and golden oldies rock.

➕ Off map at F1 ✉ 3771 Roswell Road ☎ 404/233–8026 ⏲ Sun–Fri 8PM–3AM; Sat 8PM–4AM 🚌 5

MASQUERADE

This tri-level club, whose three separate spaces are known as Heaven, Hell, and Purgatory, appeals to a diverse crowd with its eclectic mix of popular music, disco, techno, and industrial rock. The open floor in front of the bands is often crowded with dancers.

➕ H5 ✉ 695 North Avenue ☎ 404/577–8178 ⏲ Mon–Sat 8PM–2AM 🚌 2, 27, 46, 99

SOMBER REPTILE

Housed in a dingy Downtown warehouse, this club plays to youthful angst with loud, hard-core punk, grunge, ska, and industrial rock from local and regional bands. Not for the timid.

➕ D4 ✉ 842 Marietta Street ☎ 404/577–8178 ⏲ Daily 9PM–1AM 🚇 Omni/Dome/GWCC (W1) 🚌 1, 26, 50

SPECTATOR SPORTS

ATLANTA BRAVES

The National League's Braves, the 1995 World Champions, tried to repeat their success in 1996, but were defeated in six games by the American League's New York Yankees. They currently play their home games at Atlanta-Fulton County Stadium, where Hall of Fame star Hank Aaron broke Babe Ruth's record of 714 home runs (April 8, 1974). In 1997 the Braves occupied Olympic Stadium, built for the 1996 Centennial Olympic Games, and since converted to a baseball stadium seating 45,000–48,000 people.

➕ F8 ✉ 521 Capitol Avenue
☎ Ticketmaster:
404/249–6400. 404/522–7630
🕐 Main season: mid-Apr–Oct
Ⓜ Georgia State (E1)
🚌 Shuttle bus from Five Points station (O) for baseball games, or 17, 55, 90, 97, 100

ATLANTA FALCONS

The Falcons give Atlantans a chance to see professional football. Overall, the team has been a disappointment, usually playing .500 ball and not making the playoffs. The best part is seeing a game in the Georgia Dome with 70,000-plus other screaming, chanting fans.

➕ E6 ✉ Georgia Dome
(► 78) ☎ 404/223–8000
🕐 Main season: Sep–Jan
Ⓜ Omni/Dome/GWCC (W1)
🚌 13, 51, 63

ATLANTA HAWKS

The Hawks play in the central division of the National Basketball Association eastern conference. Since this is in the same division as the superior Chicago Bulls, it is rare for the Hawks to win a division championship, though they usually end up in the conference playoffs.

➕ E6 ✉ Omni Coliseum
(► 78) ☎ Ticketmaster:
404/249–6400.
404/827–DUNK 🕐 Main season: Oct–Apr
Ⓜ Omni/Dome/GWCC (W1)
🚌 1, 11, 13, 18, 26, 50, 86

ATLANTA INTERNATIONAL RACEWAY

Hampton (20 miles south of Atlanta) is the site of several NASCAR stock-car race events, including the Coca-Cola 500 (March) and Atlanta Journal 500 (November). They feature famous drivers such as Georgia's own Bill Elliott, plus the likes of Kyle Petty and Darrell Waltrip.

➕ Off map at D13
✉ Hampton, Georgia (follow signs) ☎ 404/946–4211
🕐 Call for events schedule
❓ Accessible only by car

GEORGIA TECH YELLOW JACKETS

Participating in the NCAA's tough Atlantic Coast Conference, Georgia Tech teams give you high-quality collegiate football (1990 national champion), basketball, baseball, tennis, wrestling, and other sports.

➕ F4/5 ✉ Georgia Institute of Technology campus (between North Avenue and 10th Street)
☎ 404/894–5447
Ⓜ North Avenue (N3) 🚌 13

Annual sporting events

Atlanta is host to several annual sporting events, including the Peachtree Road Race run on July 4 (14km); the Bell South Atlanta Classic, a four-day tournament with the world's best golfers (May; ☎ 404/951–8777); and the AT&T Challenge, a tennis tournament featuring the world's top-ranked men players (April; ☎ 404/881–8811).

LUXURY HOTELS

Modern luxury

The majority of Atlanta's most expensive establishments are in Downtown and Buckhead, with a few in Midtown and along the north perimeter of the city. Architecturally, all are modern, the oldest being the Hyatt Regency Atlanta which opened in 1967. All are owned by international hotel chains. You can expect to pay $160 or more for a double or twin-bedded room.

ATLANTA MARRIOTT MARQUIS

Downtown's newest luxury hotel (► 50) is the largest in Atlanta, with 1,671 rooms. The hotel has an efficient staff and numerous amenities, including five restaurants and a health club.
🟥 F6 ✉ 265 Peachtree Center Avenue ☎ 404/521–0000 or 800/328–9290; fax 404/586–6299 🚇 Peachtree Center (N1) 🚌 16, 31, 46

GRAND HOTEL

This elegant hotel offers affordable luxury with its lavish marble-tiled atrium lobby, two outstanding restaurants and spacious rooms.
🟥 F3 ✉ 75 14th Street ☎ 404/881–9898 or 800/952–0702; fax 404/873–4692 🚇 Arts Center (N5) 🚌 98

HOTEL NIKKO ATLANTA

A bi-level lobby facing a courtyard with a Japanese garden and 35-foot waterfall invites you into this hotel. Its two restaurants (Mediterranean French and Japanese cuisine) are among the city's best.
🟥 Off map at H1 ✉ 3300 Peachtree Road at Piedmont Road ☎ 404/365–8100 or 800/645–5687; fax 404/233–5686 🚇 Buckhead (N7), Lenox (NE7) 🚌 5, 23

OMNI HOTEL AT CNN CENTER

This hotel is in a prime location if you are attending events at the World Congress Center, Omni Coliseum or Georgia Dome. A MARTA station next to the Coliseum puts other Atlanta sights just a few minutes away.
🟥 F6 ✉ 100 CNN Center ☎ 404/659–0000 or 800/843–6664; fax 404/525–5050 🚇 Omni/Dome/WCC (W1) 🚌 1, 11, 13, 18, 26, 50, 86

RITZ-CARLTON ATLANTA

With its coolly efficient service, the Ritz reminds you of the best luxury hotels. Rooms are spacious and pleasantly furnished with reproduction antiques.
🟥 F6 ✉ 181 Peachtree Street ☎ 404/659–0400 or 800/241–3333; fax 404/688–0400 🚇 Peachtree Center (N1) 🚌 10, 31

RITZ-CARLTON BUCKHEAD

Decorated with antiques, this elegant hotel offers excellent service, style and location. Lenox Square Mall and Phipps Plaza are both opposite. The hotel Dining Room is one of the U.S.'s best restaurants (► 66).
🟥 Off map at K1 ✉ 3434 Peachtree Road ☎ 404/237–2700 or 800/241–3333; fax 404/239–0078 🚇 Buckhead (N7), Lenox (NE7) 🚌 23, 25, 47, 48, 85, 92, 140

WESTIN PEACHTREE PLAZA HOTEL

This 73-story, cylindrical glass tower is the second-tallest hotel in North America. Rooms above the 40th story offer great views of Downtown.
🟥 F6 ✉ 210 Peachtree Street ☎ 404/659–1400 or 800/228–3000; fax 404/589–7424 🚇 Peachtree Center (N1) 🚌 10, 13, 31

MID-RANGE HOTELS

ANSLEY INN

This handsome three-story brick Tudor mansion, now used as a bed-and-breakfast, has oversize guest rooms, all with private baths and decorated with Chinese porcelains and antiques.

✚ G3 ✉ 253 15th Street ☎ 404/872–9000 or 800/446–5416; fax 404/892–2318 🚇 Arts Center (N5) 🚌 10, 31, 36

BEST WESTERN INN AT THE PEACHTREE

A bargain in an expensive area. The attractive rooms in this small Downtown hotel are furnished with extra chairs, a sofa and a walk-in wardrobe. A complimentary Continental breakfast is also served.

✚ F6 ✉ 330 West Peachtree Street ☎ 404/577–6970 or 800/528–1234 🚇 Peachtree Center (N1) 🚌 10, 31, 46

DAYS INN HOTEL– PEACHTREE

Located opposite the Fox Theatre, this 12-story hotel is a bargain, if only for its location. Housed in a 1924 former luxury apartment building, it has a sumptuous lobby with an 18th-century Georgian brass chandelier suspended from a lofty mahogany-panelled ceiling, and there are reproduction antiques in the rooms.

✚ F4 ✉ 683 Peachtree Street ☎ 404/874–9200 or 800/325–2525; fax 404/873–4245 🚇 North Avenue (N3) 🚌 2, 10, 45

DOUBLETREE HOTEL ATLANTA

This ultramodern hotel on the northern perimeter of Atlanta gives a taste of luxury at an affordable price (high end of the moderate range). Its spacious rooms, efficient service, and first-class restaurant, plus privileges for all its guests at a nearby fitness club, make it a popular choice.

✚ Off map at G1 ✉ Seven Concourse Parkway ☎ 404/395–3900 or 800/222–TREE; fax 404/395–3935 🚇 Dunwoody (N9) 🚌 150

RESIDENCE INN MIDTOWN BY MARRIOTT

This suites-only hotel resembles a classy apartment building. Each unit has a fully equipped kitchen, comfortable reproduction antique furniture, full-length mirrors, marble-tiled bathrooms, ceiling fans, and a television in every room. A Continental breakfast is served off the lobby.

✚ F3 ✉ 1041 West Peachtree Street ☎ 404/872–8885 or 800/331–3131; fax 404/872–8888 🚇 Midtown (N4) 🚌 37

TERRACE GARDEN INN BUCKHEAD

This stylish hotel is in a prime location opposite Lenox Square Mall. Its comfortable rooms contain reproduction French and English antique furniture, and it has a fitness area, a swimming pool, and tennis courts.

✚ Off map at K1 ✉ 3405 Lenox Road ☎ 404/261–9250 or 800/241–8260; fax 404/848–7301 🚇 Lenox (NE7) 🚌 23, 25, 47, 48, 85, 92, 140

Hotel choice

Finding a hotel in Atlanta shouldn't be a problem, but don't expect a room without an advance reservation if you want to stay in Downtown, Midtown, or Buckhead, since these areas together form the prime turf of business people and those attending conventions. As an alternative, consider the north "Perimeter" (along I-285 between I-75 and I-85), which has several excellent hotels in all price categories and sizes. On average, you can expect to pay $85–$159 for a double or twin-bedded room.

BUDGET ACCOMMODATIONS

Motel rooms

Inexpensive lodging in Atlanta is also available from several national motel chains, nondescript one- to four-story structures usually bordering the interstate highways. Double-occupancy rooms with private baths, one large bed or two double beds, a television, desk, and other basic amenities are in the $50–$80 range.

BEST WESTERN AMERICAN HOTEL

Though on the high end of the inexpensive range, this older hotel—opposite the bus station and behind the gleaming Westin Peachtree Plaza Hotel—is an excellent choice if you are seeking a good location and value for money. Famous guests who stayed here before more modern alternatives were built include Elvis Presley and Richard Nixon.

✠ F6 ✉ 160 Spring Street ☎ 404/688–8600; fax 404/658–9458 🚇 Peachtree Center (N1) 🚌 13

CHESHIRE MOTOR INN

This family-run motor lodge, located between Downtown and Buckhead, is a favorite for its inexpensive prices and personal touches, such as free coffee and newspapers every morning. The Colonnade Restaurant (▶ 62), one of the best for southern cuisine, is on the same premises.

✠ Off map at H1 ✉ 1865 Cheshire Bridge Road ☎ 404/872–9628 or 800/827–9628; fax 404/875–0640 🚌 27

EMORY INN

This older hotel, tucked into a forest near Emory University, provides a peaceful setting away from the hustle and bustle of the commercial business districts, yet still lies only a short drive away from all the action.

✠ Off map at K2 ✉ 1641 Clifton Road ☎ 404/712–6700 or 800/933–6679; fax 404/712–6701 🚌 6

HAMPTON INN BUCKHEAD

Although the Hampton's rooms are neither large nor fancy, the location and price are right, plus there's an indoor pool and an all-you-can-eat Continental breakfast held in the lobby every morning. This chain also guarantees your stay: if you're not 100 percent satisfied, they'll refund your money.

✠ Off map at H1 ✉ 3398 Piedmont Road ☎ 404/233–5656 or 800/HAMPTON; fax 404/237–4688 🚇 Buckhead (N7) 🚌 5

LENOX INN

This attractive motel, opposite Lenox Square Mall, assures you of good service at a very affordable price. The rooms are basic, but clean and well furnished with modern amenities. The fitness room and exercise facilities of the adjacent Terrace Garden Inn are also available to guests of the Lenox.

✠ Off map at K1 ✉ 3387 Lenox Road ☎ 404/261–5500 or 800/578–7878; fax 404/261–6140 🚇 Lenox (NE7) 🚌 23, 25, 47, 48, 85, 92, 140

QUALITY HOTEL

This older hotel, with tastefully decorated rooms, is located a few blocks from Peachtree Street, and is convenient for Downtown sights. Its Celebrity Café is renowned for its waffles and fried chicken.

✠ F6 ✉ 89 Luckie Street ☎ 404/524–7991; fax 404/525–0672 🚇 Peachtree Center (N1) 🚌 13

ATLANTA
travel facts

ARRIVING & DEPARTING

When to go

- Spring and fall are the best seasons.
- April is "blossom time" for a wide range of shrubs, trees, and flowers.
- October temperatures are moderate and the city is once again filled with color as the tree leaves change from green to brilliant shades of red, orange, and yellow.
- Most outdoor arts and crafts fairs are held from mid-September to mid-November.

Climate

- Average summer temperatures range from 83°F to 88°F, often with 80–90 per cent humidity.
- Winter temperatures rarely dip below 40°F during the day, but with higher humidity the dampness often makes it seem colder. Snow and ice are rare.
- Spring and autumn temperatures are 65–84°F during the day.
- There are violent thunderstorms in late spring and summer.
- For the weather forecast, temperature and time ☎ 404/455–7141.

Arriving by air

- The major gateway to Atlanta is Hartsfield Atlanta International Airport (☎ 404/530–6830), one of the busiest airports in the U.S.
- Hartsfield has daily nonstop flights to 150 domestic destinations.
- An automated, high-speed, mini-subway train links the arrival concourses to the main terminal building and baggage area. Moving sidewalks link the concourse subway waiting areas.
- Transportation into the city is provided by the MARTA Rapid Rail system (➤ 91), taxis, shuttle buses, and rental-car companies.
- Major American carriers serving Atlanta include:

America West ☎ 800/235–9292.
American ☎ 800/433–7300.
Air South ☎ 800/247–7688.
Continental ☎ 800/523–3273.
Delta ☎ Domestic reservations: 800/221–1212. International reservations: 800/241–4141.
Northwest ☎ 800/225–2525.
TWA ☎ 800/221–2000.
United ☎ 800/241–6522.
USAir ☎ 800/428–4322.

- For inexpensive, no-frills flights, contact Kiwi International (☎ 800/ 538–5494), based in Newark and New York; Midwest Express (☎ 800/452–2022), based in Milwaukee, which serves 45 U.S. cities in the Midwest and on both coasts, including Atlanta; and Valu-Jet (☎ 800/825–8538), based in Atlanta.

Arriving by bus and train

- Greyhound Bus Lines (✉ 81 International Boulevard ☎ 800/ 231–2222 or 404/584–1731) links Atlanta with other major U.S. cities.
- Amtrak (✉ 1688 Peachtree Street ☎ 800/872–7245) has regular services to and from Birmingham, Mobile, New Orleans, Greenville, Charlotte, Washington, D.C., Baltimore, Philadelphia, and New York.

Arriving by car

- Atlanta is easily accessible from several locations by interstate highway (see "City layout") and major highways that enter the city.
- Avoid these roads and highways during the rush hours (6:30–9AM and 3:30–7PM).

City layout

- Atlanta is circled by I-285, known by locals as the Perimeter, and crossed east–west by I-20 and north–south by I-75 and I-85.
- North of the MARTA Five Points station, Peachtree Street bisects

the city, traveling up through Downtown, Midtown and Buckhead (now Peachtree Road) to the suburb of Chamblee, just inside the north Perimeter.

ESSENTIAL FACTS

Travel insurance

- Travel insurance covering baggage, health, and trip cancellation or interruptions is available from: **Access America** ✉ Box 90315, Richmond, VA 23286 ☎ 804/285–3300 or 800/284–8300. **Carefree Travel Insurance** ✉ Box 9366, 100 Garden City Plaza, Garden City, NY 11530 ☎ 516/294–0220 or 800/323–3149. **Near Services** ✉ Box 1339, Calumet City, IL 60409 ☎ 708/868–6700 or 800/654–6700. **Tele-Trip** ✉ Mutual of Omaha Plaza, Box 31716, Omaha, NE 68131 ☎ 800/228–9792. **Travel Guard International** ✉ 1145 Clark Street, Stevens Point, WI 54481 ☎ 715/345–0505 or 800/826–1300. **Travel Insured International** ✉ Box 280568, East Hartford, CT 06128-0568 ☎ 203/528–7663 or 800/243–3174. **Wallach & Company** ✉ 107 W. Federal Street, Box 480, Middleburg, VA 22117 ☎ 703/687–3166 or 800/237–6615.

Average opening hours

- Department stores and malls: Mon–Sat 9:30–9; Sun noon–5:30.
- Specialty shops: Mon–Sat 9:30–6.
- Supermarkets: daily 24 hours (Kroger chain and others).
- Banks: Mon–Fri 9–5; Sat 9–noon for a few locations.
- Museums: Mon–Sat 10–5; Sun noon–5.
- Offices: Mon–Fri 8:30–5.

- Post offices: Mon–Fri 8:30–5; Sat 9–1 for a few locations.

Public holidays

- New Year's Day.
- Martin Luther King, Jr. Day (third Monday in January).
- President's Day (third Monday in February).
- Memorial Day (last Monday in May).
- Independence Day (July 4).
- Labor Day (first Monday in September).
- Veterans' Day (November 11).
- Thanksgiving Day (fourth Thursday in November).
- Christmas Day.
- Banks, post offices, and most government agencies are closed for these holidays, although most museums and shops are open.

Money matters

- Nearly all banks have ATMs, which accept cards registered in other countries that are linked to the Cirrus or Plus networks. Before leaving home, check which network your cards are linked to, and ensure your personal identification number is valid. For specific Cirrus locations in the United States and Canada, ☎ 800/424–7787. For U.S. Plus locations, ☎ 800/843–7587 and enter the area code and first three digits of the number you are calling from (or of the calling area where you want an ATM).
- Credit cards are a widely accepted and secure alternative to cash. Visa, MasterCard, American Express, Diner's Club, and Discover are the most common.
- Traveler's checks function like cash in all but small shops; $20 and $50 denominations are the most useful.
- Traveler's checks and foreign

currency can be exchanged at Thomas Cook-Wachovia Bank of Georgia foreign-exchange counter (⊙ Mon–Fri 9–7; Sat–Sun 4–7), directly opposite the airport's international airline ticket counters. Wachovia, NationsBank, First Union and other local banks also have foreign-exchange counters at their Downtown offices and selected branches.

- You can send or receive a MoneyGram from American Express (☎ 800/926–9400) for up to $20,000. There are MoneyGram agents in more than 70 countries. Western Union (☎ 800/325–6000) is linked to 22,000 locations in 78 countries.

Etiquette

- Southerners are generally friendly and may greet you on the street even though you are a stranger. But beware of where this happens, as Downtown is known for mug-gings and other violent crimes.
- Smoking is forbidden on public transportation and in most public buildings and shops. Restaurants usually have both smoking and nonsmoking sections.

Places of worship

- Most believers in Atlanta are Christian, divided mainly between Protestant denominations. Churches meet for worship on Sunday mornings.
- There are also places of worship for Jews and Muslims.

Student travelers

- With 36 universities and colleges, Atlanta provides numerous learning opportunities for students. Admission discounts are available with a valid student ID card at various music clubs, museums, and tourist sights.

- The Atlanta Convention and Visitors Bureau (✉ 233 Peachtree Street, Suite 2000, Atlanta, GA 30303 ☎ 800/ATLANTA or 404/222–6688) has an "International Youth Travel Program" where students are given discounted rates at 11 hotels.
- The American Youth Hostel (✉ 223 Ponce de Leon Avenue ☎ 404/872–8844) has inexpensive lodgings for students.

Travel agencies

- For names of reputable agencies in your area, contact the **American Society of Travel Agents** (✉ 1101 King Street, Suite 200, Alexandria, VA 22314 ☎ 703/739–2782).

Rest rooms

- Rest rooms are reasonably plentiful, located at all tourist sights, shopping malls, deparment stores, libraries, fast-food eateries, and restaurants. There is no charge for their use, but cleanliness does vary greatly.

Senior citizens

- Contact the **American Association of Retired Persons** (✉ AARP, 601E Street NW, Washington, DC 20049 ☎ 202/434–2277 ▦ $8 per person or couple annually) for information about member discounts and road-service aid. For other discounts on lodgings, car rentals, and other travel products, along with magazines and newsletters, contact the **National Council of Senior Citizens** (✉ 1331 F Street NW, Washington, DC 20004 ☎ 202/347–8800 ▦ Membership: $12 annually), and *Mature Outlook* magazine (✉ 6001 N. Clark Street, Chicago, IL 60660 ☎ 312/465–6466 or 800/336–6330 ▦ Subscription: $9.95 annually).

Public Transportation

- To use public transportation, look for the word MARTA (Metropolitan Atlanta Rapid Transit Association) at bus stops and train stations.
- You will find letters and numbers in brackets after the names of MARTA stops. These indicate the direction of the line and number of stops from Five Points (0), the hub of the network.

MARTA Rapid Rail

- Clean, efficient and safe "Rapid Rail" trains run beneath Downtown and Midtown Atlanta as a subway, and primarily on elevated tracks across the rest of the city.
- The east–west line stops at 14 stations from Hightower near the west side of I-285 to Indian Creek just beyond the east side of I-285; the Proctor Creek extension line branches beyond the Ashby station (W3) to one additional stop.
- The north–south line, with 17 stations, runs from Hartsfield Atlanta International Airport to Doraville, a suburb just northwest of the I-85 and I-285 intersection.
- Both main lines cross at the Downtown Five Points station, where a transfer can be made free to the other line. Station entrances, exits, platforms, and directions are clearly marked.
- The cost of a ride on a MARTA train or bus is $1.50. Station turnstiles require exact change (excluding pennies or half dollars), or tokens can be purchased from machines at the station entrance.
- For transferring to a bus line at the departure stop, push the white "Transfer" button after inserting your money in the turnstile. There is a designated slot on the turnstile to insert discount cards.

- Trains run 4:35AM–1:17AM, with 8–15 minute intervals between trains depending on the line, day and time.
- From the airport to Five Points takes 15 minutes, to Peachtree Center 17 minutes and to Lenox Square Mall 30 minutes.
- Free parking is available at most suburban stations.
- MARTA has a good security record, with its own police force. Every station is monitored by a closed-circuit television system.

MARTA buses

- MARTA operates 700 buses on 150 routes covering 1,500 miles.
- Outside of I-285, service is limited.
- Selected buses stop at most Rapid Rail stations and at hundreds of street locations.
- To identify a street bus stop, look for a 4-foot-high white cement post with "BUS STOP" carved into it; some stops also have a small covered area or bench.
- A special machine accepts $1 bills and there is a slot for coins.
- Discount pass cards must be shown to the driver upon entering the bus, and a transfer slip, if needed, must be requested from the driver.

Schedule & map information

- Schedule and route maps are available for all the MARTA rail lines and buses at the Five Points station, and are in limited stock at the other stations.
- Any other questions can be answered at the information booths manned by MARTA employees, or by phoning or writing: ✉ 2424 Piedmont Road, Atlanta, GA 30324 ☎ 404/848–4711.

Ticket discounts

- Two- and three-day weekend

passes ($6 and $8) give unlimited travel on both trains and buses.
- Weekly TransCards ($12) allow seven days of unlimited travel; monthly TransCards cost $45.
- Passes and cards can be purchased at the Ride Store at the Five Points station, and at the business offices of several area grocery stores and businesses.

Taxis
- Cabs cannot be hailed off the street in Atlanta; instead call for one or go to a hotel or MARTA station where they congregate.
- Taxi fares start at $1.50 for the first one-sixth mile and 20¢ for each additional one-sixth mile. There is a $1 charge for each additional person.
- For any destination within the Downtown Convention Zone (bounded by Boulevard, 14th Street, Northside Drive and Atlanta-Fulton County Stadium), a flat fare of $4 for one person or $2 per person for two or more passengers is charged.
- Between the airport and Downtown hotels, there is a fixed rate of $15 for one person, $8 each for two people, $6 each for three people.
- 24-hour service: Checker Cab (☎ 404/351–1111); Buckhead Safety Cab (☎ 404/233–1152).

MEDIA & COMMUNICATIONS

Telephones
- The long-distance services of AT&T (☎ 800/222–0300), MCI (☎ 800/950–5555), and Sprint (☎ 800/877–7746) make calling home relatively convenient and let you avoid hotel surcharges.
- Information ☎ 411.

Post offices
- There are more than 100 post offices in the Atlanta area.

Newspapers & magazines
- The *Atlanta Journal* is the city's daily morning newspaper and the *Atlanta Constitution* is the evening edition.
- *USA Today, Wall Street Journal,* and *New York Times* are available at some newsstands and bookstores.
- *Creative Loafing,* a weekly paper, has good information about entertainment. It is distributed free at MARTA stations, restaurants, and stores. Free monthlies include *Where Atlanta, Atlanta Now* and *Key Atlanta,* distributed by hotels and the tourism bureau.
- The monthly *Atlanta Magazine* is the official city magazine, with stories about local personalities, restaurants, fashion, and events.

Radio stations
- There are numerous commercial radio stations to choose from on both AM and FM dials, covering a gamut of musical tastes and talk show subjects.

Television
- Atlanta has a good selection of 24-hour television viewing, including the major networks—ABC, CBS, and NBC—plus the Fox Network, PBS, TBS, and several independent stations.
- Most hotels have cable television, which offers a very wide range of selections—including Atlanta's own CNN.

EMERGENCIES

Sensible precautions
- Housing projects and slums lie

adjacent to Downtown on all sides except the north; do no venture into them alone.

- Tourist sights are safe during the day, but extra caution needs to be taken at night, especially in Downtown and Midtown, and at nightclubs anywhere in the city.
- Stick to main streets, avoid parks, alleys and other isolated areas after dark, don't wear visible jewelry, and don't carry large sums of cash.
- On subway trains, sit in the first car, nearest to the driver.

Lost property
- Contact the Atlanta Police Department ☎ 404/658–6600. You will need its report for an insurance claim.

Medical treatment
- Ambulance ☎ 911.
- Hospital 24-hour emergency rooms:
  Downtown: Grady Memorial Hospital ✉ 80 Butler Street ☎ 404/616–4307.
  Midtown: Crawford Long Hospital ✉ 550 Peachtree Street N.E. ☎ 404/ 686–4411. Emergencies: 404/892–4411. Georgia Baptist Medical Center ✉ 300 Boulevard N.E. ☎ 404/265–4000. Emergencies: 404/265–4262.
  Buckhead: Piedmont Hospital ✉ 1968 Peachtree Road N.W. ☎ 404/605–5000.

Doctors and dentists
- The Medical Association of Atlanta (☎ 404/881–1714 ◷ Mon–Thu 9–4; Fri 9–3) has a referral service for over 2,000 Atlanta physicians in every field of expertise.
- The Georgia Dental Association of Atlanta (☎ 404/636–7553; ◷ Mon– Fri 8:30–5) will refer

you to a dentist closest to your hotel for any special needs.

Medicines
- 24-hour pharmacy: Revco Drug Store ✉ 1061 Ponce de Leon Avenue, ☎ 404/876–0381.
- Kroger supermarkets, a 24-hour grocery chain with over 50 Atlanta locations, have a full-service pharmacy ◷ Daily (except Christmas) 9–9.

Emergency telephone numbers
- Ambulance, fire, and police ☎ 911.
- Poison control ☎ 404/616– 9000.
- Rape crisis ☎ 404/616–4861.

Visitor Information

- Contact the **Atlanta Convention & Visitors Bureau** (✉ ACVB, 233 Peachtree Street, Suite 2000, GA 30303 ☎ 404/521–6600 or 800/ATLANTA. Automated information service: 404/222–6688) for a city map and brochures about all major sights and upcoming events. Ask for the EXPLOR-A-CARD, which can be used for discounts at selected sights, hotels, restaurants, and shops.
- The **Georgia Department of Industry, Trade and Tourism** (✉ Box 1776, GA 30301 ☎ 404/656–3590 or 800/847–4842; fax 404/656–3567) can answer most of your questions about travel in the state.
- The free *Georgia on My Mind* magazine offers a wealth of information.
- The **Welcome South Visitors Center** (✉ 200 Spring Street ☎ 404/224–2000) has information and exhibits about Atlanta and the region, as well as a Thomas Cook office, AAA Club South, and other services.

INDEX

Citypack
Atlanta

Published in the United States by Fodor's Travel Publications, Inc.
Published in the United Kingdom by AA Publishing

Fodor's is a registered trademark of Fodor's Travel Publications, Inc.

ISBN 0–679–00000–3
Second Edition

FODOR'S CITYPACK ATLANTA

AUTHOR *Mark Beffart*
CARTOGRAPHY *The Automobile Association
RV Reise- und Verkehrsverlag*
COVER DESIGN *Tigist Getachew, Fabrizio La Rocca*
COPY EDITOR *Lynn Bresler*
VERIFIER *Giselle Rothwell*
INDEXER *Marie Lorimer*
SECOND EDITION UPDATED BY *OutHouse Publishing Services*

Acknowledgments

The Automobile Association would like to thank the following photographers, libraries and associations for their assistance in the preparation of this book:
THE ATLANTA CYCLORAMA (T WARREN) 12, 25a; ATLANTA LANDMARKS 1994 (KEVIN C ROSE) 7; CENTER FOR PUPPETRY ARTS 5a, 45; REX FEATURES LTD 9; THE SCIENCE & TECHNOLOGY MUSEUM OF ATLANTA 39a; SOUTHEASTERN RAILWAY MUSEUM 54.
All remaining pictures are held in the Association's own library (AA PHOTO LIBRARY), and were taken by ETHEL DAVIES.

Special sales

Color separation by Daylight Colour Art Pte Ltd, Singapore
Manufactured by Dai Nippon Printing Co. (Hong Kong) Ltd
10 9 8 7 6 5 4 3 2 1

Titles in the Citypack series
● Amsterdam ● Atlanta ● Berlin ● Boston ● Chicago ● Florence ● Hong Kong ●
● London ● Los Angeles ● Miami ● Montréal ● New York ● Paris ● Prague ●
● Rome ● San Francisco ● Tokyo ● Toronto ● Venice ● Washington, D.C. ●